Oakland Athletics 2020

A Baseball Companion

Edited by R.J. Anderson, Craig Goldstein and Bret Sayre

Baseball Prospectus

Craig Brown, Steven Goldman and David Pease, Consultant Editors
Robert Au, Harry Pavlidis and Amy Pircher, Statistics Editors

Copyright © 2020 by DIY Baseball, LLC.
All rights reserved

This book or any part thereof may not be reproduced or transmitted in any form or by any means, electronic or mechanical, including photocopying, recording, or by any information storage and retrieval system, without permission in writing from the publisher.

Limit of Liability/Disclaimer of Warranty: While the publisher and the author have used their best efforts in preparing this book, they make no representations or warranties with respect to the accuracy or completeness of the contents of this book and specifically disclaim any implied warranties of merchantability or fitness for a particular purpose. No warranty may be created or extended by sales representatives or written sales materials. The advice and strategies contained herein may not be suitable for your situation. You should consult with a professional where appropriate. Neither the publisher nor the author shall be liable for any loss of profit or any other commercial damages, including but not limited to special, incidental, consequential, or other damages.

Library of Congress Cataloging-in-Publication Data:
paperback
ISBN-13: 978-1-949332-84-1

Project Credits
Cover Design: Michael Byzewski at Aesthetic Apparatus
Interior Design and Production: Jeff Pease, Dave Pease
Layout: Jeff Pease, Dave Pease

Baseball icon courtesy of Uberux, from https://www.shareicon.net/author/uberux

Ballpark diagram courtesy of Lou Spirito/THIRTY81 Project, https://thirty81project.com/

Manufactured in the United States of America
10 9 8 7 6 5 4 3 2 1

Table of Contents

Statistical Introduction v

Part 1: Team Analysis

Oakland A's: Where Are You Going, Where Have You Been? 3
  Craig Brown, Wilson Karaman and Matthew Trueblood
Performance Graphs 7
2019 Team Performance 8
2020 Team Projections 9
Team Personnel 10
Oakland–Alameda County Coliseum Stats 11
Athletics Team Analysis 13

Part 2: Player Analysis

Athletics Player Analysis 18
Athletics Prospects 91

Part 3: Featured Articles

The Baseball Is Juiced (Again) 109
  Robert Arthur
The Moral Hazard of Playing It Safe 113
  Craig Goldstein

Index of Names 119

Statistical Introduction

Sports are, fundamentally, a blend of athletic endeavor and storytelling. Baseball, like any other sport, tells its stories in so many ways: in the arc of a game from the stands or a season from the box scores, in photos, or even in numbers. At Baseball Prospectus, we understand that statistics don't replace observation or any of baseball's stories, but complement everything else that makes the game so much fun.

What stats help us with is with patterns and precision, variance and value. This book can help you learn things you may not see from watching a game or hundred, whether it's the path of a career over time or the breadth of the entire MLB. We'd also never ask you to choose between our numbers and the experience of viewing a game from the cheap seats or the comfort of your home; our publication combines running the numbers with observations and wisdom from some of the brightest minds we can find. But if you *do* want to learn more about the numbers beyond what's on the backs of player jerseys, let us help explain.

Offense

We've revised our methodology for determining batting value. Long-time readers of the book will notice that we've retired True Average in favor of a new metric: Deserved Runs Created Plus (DRC+). Developed by Jonathan Judge and our stats team, this statistic measures everything a player does at the plate–reaching base, hitting for power, making outs, and moving runners over–and puts it on a scale where 100 equals league-average performance. A DRC+ of 150 is terrific, a DRC+ of 100 is average and a DRC+ of 75 means you better be an excellent defender.

DRC+ also does a better job than any of our previous metrics in taking contextual factors into account. The model adjusts for how the park affects performance, but also for things like the talent of the opposing pitcher, value of different types of batted-ball events, league, temperature and other factors. It's able to describe a player's expected offensive contribution than any other statistic we've found over the years, and also does a better job of predicting future performance as well.

There's a lot more to DRC+'s story, and you can read all about it in greater depth near the end of this book.

Oakland Athletics 2020

The other aspect of run-scoring is baserunning, which we quantify using Baserunning Runs. BRR not only records the value of stolen bases (or getting caught in the act), but also accounts for all the stuff that doesn't show up on the back of a baseball card: a runner's ability to go first to third on a single, or advance on a fly ball.

Defense

Where offensive value is *relatively* easy to identify and understand, defensive value is…not. Over the past dozen years, the sabermetric community has focused mostly on stats based on zone data: a real-live human person records the type of batted ball and estimated landing location, and models are created that give expected outs. From there, you can compare fielders' actual outs to those expected ones. Simple, right?

Unfortunately, zone data has two major issues. First, zone data is recorded by commercial data providers who keep the raw data private unless you pay for it. (All the statistics we build in this book and on our website use public data as inputs.) That hurts our ability to test assumptions or duplicate results. Second, over the years it has become apparent that there's quite a bit of "noise" in zone-based fielding analysis. Sometimes the conclusions drawn from zone data don't hold up to scrutiny, and sometimes the different data provided by different providers don't look anything alike, giving wildly different results. Sometimes the hard-working professional stringers or scorers might unknowingly inflict unconscious bias into the mix: for example good fielders will often be credited with more expected outs despite the data, and ballparks with high press boxes tend to score more line drives than ones with a lower press box.

Enter our Fielding Runs Above Average (FRAA). For most positions, FRAA is built from play-by-play data, which allows us to avoid the subjectivity found in many other fielding metrics. The idea is this: count how many fielding plays are made by a given player and compare that to expected plays for an average fielder at their position (based on pitcher ground ball tendencies and batter handedness). Then we adjust for park and base-out situations.

When it comes to catchers, our methodology is a little different thanks to the laundry list of responsibilities they're tasked with beyond just, well, catching and throwing the ball. By now you've probably heard about "framing" or the art of making umpires more likely to call balls outside the strike zone for strikes. To put this into one tidy number, we incorporate pitch tracking data (for the years it exists) and adjust for important factors like pitcher, umpire, batter and home-field advantage using a mixed-model approach. This grants us a number for how many strikes the catcher is personally adding to (or subtracting from) his pitchers' performance…which we then convert to runs added or lost using linear weights.

Framing is one of the biggest parts of determining catcher value, but we also take into account blocking balls from going past, whether a scorer deems it a passed ball or a wild pitch. We use a similar approach—one that really benefits from the pitch tracking data that tells us what ends up in the dirt and what doesn't. We also include a catcher's ability to prevent stolen bases and how well they field balls in play, and *finally* we come up with our FRAA for catchers.

Pitching

Both pitching and fielding make up the half of baseball that isn't run scoring: run prevention. Separating pitching from fielding is a tough task, and most recent pitching analysis has branched off from Voros McCracken's famous (and controversial) statement, "There is little if any difference among major-league pitchers in their ability to prevent hits on balls hit in the field of play." The research of the analytic community has validated this to some extent, and there are a host of "defense-independent" pitching measures that have been developed to try and extract the effect of the defense behind a hurler from the pitcher's work.

Our solution to this quandary is Deserved Run Average (DRA), our core pitching metric. DRA looks like earned run average (ERA), the tried-and-true pitching stat you've seen on every baseball broadcast or box score from the past century, but it's very different. To start, DRA takes an event-by-event look at what the pitchers does, and adjusts the value of that event based on different environmental factors like park, batter, catcher, umpire, base-out situation, run differential, inning, defense, home field advantage, pitcher role and temperature. That mixed model gives us a pitcher's expected contribution, similar to what we do for our DRC+ model for hitters and FRAA model for catchers. (Oh, and we also consider the pitcher's effect on basestealing and on balls getting past the catcher.)

It's important to note that DRA is set to the scale of runs allowed per nine innings (RA9) instead of ERA, which makes DRA's scale slightly higher than ERA's. The reason for this is because ERA tends to overrate three types of pitchers:

1. Pitchers who play in parks where scorers hand out more errors. Official scorers differ significantly in the frequency at which they assign errors to fielders.
2. Ground-ball pitchers, because a substantial proportion of errors occur on groundballs.
3. Pitchers who aren't very good. Better pitchers often allow fewer unearned runs than bad pitchers, because good pitchers tend to find ways to get out of jams.

Since the last time you picked up an edition of this book, we've also made a few minor changes to DRA to make it better. Recent research into "tunneling"—the act of throwing consecutive pitches that appear similar from a batter's point of view until after the swing decision point–data has given us a new contextual factor to account for in DRA: plate distance. This refers to the distance between successive pitches as they approach the plate, and while it has a smaller effect than factors like velocity or whiff rate, it still can help explain pitcher strikeout rate in our model.

New Pitching Metrics for 2020

We're including a few "new" pitching metrics in the book for the 2020 edition, though unlike last year, these numbers may be a little bit more familiar to those of you who have spent some time investigating baseball statistics.

Fastball Percentage

Our fastball percentage (FB%) statistic measures how frequently a pitcher throws a pitch classified as a "fastball," measured as a percentage of overall pitches thrown. We qualify three types of fastballs:

1. The traditional four-seam fastball;
2. The two-seam fastball or sinker;
3. "Hard cutters," which are pitches that have the movement profile of a cut fastball and are used as the pitcher's primary offering or in place of a more traditional fastball.

For example, a pitcher with a FB% of 67 throws any combination of these three pitches about two-thirds of the time.

Whiff Rate

Everybody loves a swing and a miss, and whiff rate (WHF) measures how frequently pitchers induce a swinging strike. To calculate WHF, we add up all the pitches thrown that ended with a swinging strike, then divide that number by a pitcher's total pitches thrown. Most often, high whiff rates correlate with high strikeout rates (and overall effective pitcher performance).

Called Strike Probability

Called Strike Probability (CSP) is a number that represents the likelihood that all of a pitcher's pitches will be called a strike while controlling for location, pitcher and batter handedness, umpire and count. Here's how it works: on each pitch, our model determines how many times (out of 100) that a similar pitch was called for a strike given those factors mentioned above, and when normalized for each batter's strike zone. Then we average the CSP for all pitches thrown by a pitcher in a season, and that gives us the yearly CSP percentage you see in the stats boxes.

As you might imagine, pitchers with a higher CSP are more likely to work in the zone, where pitchers with a lower CSP are likely locating their pitches outside the normal strike zone, for better or for worse.

Projections

Many of you aren't turning to this book just for a look at what a player has done, but for a look at what a player is going to do: the PECOTA projections. PECOTA, initially developed by Nate Silver (who has moved on to greater fame as a political analyst), consists of three parts:

1. Major-league equivalencies, which use minor-league statistics to project how a player will perform in the major leagues;
2. Baseline forecasts, which use weighted averages and regression to the mean to estimate a player's current true talent level; and
3. Aging curves, which uses the career paths of comparable players to estimate how a player's statistics are likely to change over time.

With all those important things covered, let's take a look at what's in the book this year.

Team Prospectus

Most of this book is composed of team chapters, with one for each of the 30 major-league franchises. On the first page of each chapter, you'll see a box that contains some of the key statistics for each team as well as a very inviting stadium diagram. (You can see an example of this for the Milwaukee Brewers on this very page!)

We start with the team name, their unadjusted 2019 win-loss record, and their divisional ranking. Beneath that are a host of other team statistics. **Pythag** presents an adjusted 2019 winning percentage, calculated by taking runs scored per game (**RS/G**) and runs allowed per game (**RA/G**) for the team, and running them through a version of Bill James' Pythagorean formula that was refined and improved by David Smyth and Brandon Heipp. (The formula is called "Pythagenpat," which is equally fun to type and to say.)

Next up is **DRC+**, described earlier, to indicate the overall hitting ability of the team either above or below league-average. Run prevention on the pitching side is covered by **DRA** (also mentioned earlier) and another metric: Fielding Independent Pitching (**FIP**), which calculates another ERA-like statistic based on strikeouts, walks, and home runs recorded. Defensive Efficiency Rating (**DER**) tells us the percentage of balls in play turned into outs for the team, and is a quick fielding shorthand that rounds out run prevention.

After that, we have several measures related to roster composition, as opposed to on-field performance. **B-Age** and **P-Age** tell us the average age of a team's batters and pitchers, respectively. **Salary** is the combined team payroll for all on-field players, and Doug Pappas' Marginal Dollars per Marginal Win (**M$/MW**) tells us how much money a team spent to earn production above replacement level.

Ending this batch of statistics is the number of disabled list days a team had over the season (**IL Days**) and the amount of salary paid to players on the disabled list (**$ on IL**); this final number is expressed as a percentage of total payroll.

Next to each of these stats, we've listed each team's MLB rank in that category from first to 30th. In this, first always indicates a positive outcome and 30th a negative outcome, except in the case of salary—first is highest.

After the franchise statistics, we share a few items about the team's home ballpark. There's the aforementioned diagram of the park's dimensions (including distances to the outfield wall), a graphic showing the height of the wall from the left-field pole to the right-field pole, and a table showing three-year park factors for the stadium. The park factors are displayed as indexes where 100 is average, 110 means that the park inflates the statistic in question by 10 percent, and 90 means that the park deflates the statistic in question by 10 percent.

On the second page of each team chapter, you'll find three graphs. The first is the **2019 Hit List Ranking**. This shows our Hit List Rank for the team on each day of the 2019 season and is intended to give you a picture of the ups and downs of the team's season. Hit List Rank measures overall team performance and drives the Hit List Power Rankings at the baseballprospectus.com website.

The second graph is **Committed Payroll** and helps you see how the team's payroll has compared to the MLB and divisional average payrolls over time. Payroll figures are current as of January 1, 2020; with so many free agents still unsigned as of this writing, the final 2020 figure will likely be significantly different for many teams. (In the meantime, you can always find the most current data at Baseball Prospectus' Cot's Baseball Contracts page.)

The third graph is **Farm System Ranking** and displays how the Baseball Prospectus prospect team has ranked the organization's farm system since 2007.

After the graphs, we have a **Personnel** section that lists many of the important decision-makers and upper-level field and operations staff members for the franchise, as well as any former Baseball Prospectus staff members who are currently part of the organization. (In very rare circumstances, someone might be on both lists!)

Juan Soto LF

Born: 10/25/98 Age: 21 Bats: L Throws: L
Height: 6'1" Weight: 185 Origin: International Free Agent, 2015

YEAR	TEAM	LVL	AGE	PA	R	2B	3B	HR	RBI	BB	K	SB	CS	AVG/OBP/SLG
2017	NAT	RK	18	27	3	1	1	0	4	2	1	0	0	.320/.370/.440
2017	HAG	A	18	96	15	5	0	3	14	10	8	1	2	.360/.427/.523
2018	HAG	A	19	74	12	5	3	5	24	14	13	2	0	.373/.486/.814
2018	POT	A+	19	73	17	3	1	7	18	11	8	0	1	.371/.466/.790
2018	HAR	AA	19	35	4	2	0	2	10	4	7	1	0	.323/.400/.581
2018	WAS	MLB	19	494	77	25	1	22	70	79	99	5	2	.292/.406/.517
2019	WAS	MLB	20	659	110	32	5	34	110	108	132	12	1	.282/.401/.548
2020	WAS	MLB	21	630	92	30	3	35	102	85	123	5	2	.284/.382/.543

Comparables: Ronald Acuña Jr., Mike Trout, Tony Conigliaro

YEAR	TEAM	LVL	AGE	PA	DRC+	VORP	BABIP	BRR	FRAA	WARP
2017	NAT	RK	18	27	135	1.5	.333	0.0	RF(9): -1.1	0.0
2017	HAG	A	18	96	181	8.0	.373	1.0	RF(19): -1.9, LF(2): -0.3	0.9
2018	HAG	A	19	74	222	14.5	.405	0.3	RF(14): 1.1, CF(2): 0.2	1.2
2018	POT	A+	19	73	260	15.4	.340	1.4	RF(14): 1.0, LF(1): 0.0	1.6
2018	HAR	AA	19	35	113	3.6	.364	0.0	LF(4): 0.6, RF(4): -0.5	0.1
2018	WAS	MLB	19	494	125	40.5	.338	-0.5	LF(114): 2.7	3.0
2019	WAS	MLB	20	659	136	49.0	.312	1.4	LF(150): -0.8	4.9
2020	WAS	MLB	21	630	133	43.6	.310	-0.1	LF 3	4.8

Position Players

After all that information and a thoughtful bylined essay covering each team, we present our player comments. These are also bylined, but due to frequent franchise shifts during the offseason, our bylines are more a rough guide than a perfect accounting of who wrote what.

Each player is listed with the major-league team that employed him as of early January 2020. If a player changed teams after that point via free agency, trade, or any other method, you'll be able to find them in the chapter for their previous squad.

As an example, take a look at the player comment for Nationals outfielder Juan Soto: the stat block that accompanies his written comment is at the top of this page. First we cover biographical information (age is as of June 30, 2020) before moving onto the stats themselves. Our statistic columns include standard identifying information like **YEAR**, **TEAM**, **LVL** (level of affiliated play) and **AGE** before getting into the numbers. Next, we provide raw, untranslated numbers like you might find on the back of your dad's baseball cards: **PA** (plate appearances), **R** (runs), **2B** (doubles), **3B** (triples), **HR** (home runs), **RBI** (runs batted in), **BB** (walks), **K** (strikeouts), **SB** (stolen bases) and **CS** (caught stealing).

Oakland Athletics 2020

Next, we have unadjusted "slash" statistics: **AVG** (batting average), **OBP** (on-base percentage) and **SLG** (slugging percentage). Following the slash line is **DRC+** (Deserved Runs Created Plus), which we described earlier as total offensive expected contribution compared to the league average.

One of our oldest active metrics, **VORP** (Value Over Replacement Player), considers offensive production, position and plate appearances. In essence, it is the number of runs contributed beyond what a replacement-level player at the same position would contribute if given the same percentage of team plate appearances. VORP does not consider the quality of a player's defense.

BABIP (batting average on balls in play) tells us how often a ball in play fell for a hit, and can help us identify whether a batter may have been lucky or not…but note that high BABIPs also tend to follow the great hitters of our time, as well as speedy singles hitters who put the ball on the ground.

The next item is **BRR** (Baserunning Runs), which covers all of a player's baserunning accomplishments including (but not limited to) swiped bags and failed attempts. Next is **FRAA** (Fielding Runs Above Average), which also includes the number of games previously played at each position noted in parentheses. Multi-position players have only their two most frequent positions listed here, but their total FRAA number reflects all positions played.

Our last column here is **WARP** (Wins Above Replacement Player). WARP estimates the total value of a player, which means for hitters it takes into account hitting runs above average (calculated using the DRC+ model), BRR and FRAA. Then, it makes an adjustment for positions played and gives the player a credit for plate appearances based upon the difference between "replacement level"—which is derived from the quality of players added to a team's roster after the start of the season–and the league average.

The final line just below the stats box is **PECOTA** data, which is discussed further in a following section.

Catchers

Catchers are a special breed, and thus they have earned their own separate box which displays some of the defensive metrics that we've built just for them. As an example, let's check out J.T. Realmuto.

The **YEAR** and **TEAM** columns match what you'd find in the other stat box. **P. COUNT** indicates the number of pitches thrown while the catcher was behind the plate, including swinging strikes, fouls and balls in play. **FRM RUNS** is the total run value the catcher provided (or cost) his team by influencing the umpire to call strikes where other catchers did not. **BLK RUNS** expresses the total run value above or below average for the catcher's ability to prevent wild pitches and passed balls. **THRW RUNS** is calculated using a similar model as the previous two statistics, and it measures a catcher's ability to throw out basestealers but also to dissuade them from testing his arm in the first place. It takes into account factors like the pitcher (including his delivery and pickoff move) and baserunner (who could be as fast as Billy Hamilton or as slow as Yonder Alonso). **TOT RUNS** is the sum of all of the previous three statistics.

Justin Verlander   RHP
Born: 02/20/83   Age: 37   Bats: R   Throws: R
Height: 6'5"   Weight: 225   Origin: Round 1, 2004 Draft (#2 overall)

YEAR	TEAM	LVL	AGE	W	L	SV	G	GS	IP	H	HR	BB/9	K/9	K	GB%	BABIP
2017	DET	MLB	34	10	8	0	28	28	172	153	23	3.5	9.2	176	34%	.283
2017	HOU	MLB	34	5	0	0	5	5	34	17	4	1.3	11.4	43	32%	.194
2018	HOU	MLB	35	16	9	0	34	34	214	156	28	1.6	12.2	290	31%	.272
2019	HOU	MLB	36	21	6	0	34	34	223	137	36	1.7	12.1	300	36%	.219
2020	HOU	MLB	37	15	6	0	29	29	184	138	28	2.3	12.1	248	35%	.274

Comparables: Zack Greinke, A.J. Burnett, Aníbal Sánchez

YEAR	TEAM	LVL	AGE	WHIP	ERA	DRA	WARP	MPH	FB%	WHF	CSP
2017	DET	MLB	34	1.28	3.82	4.03	3.0	97.7	58	11	47.8
2017	HOU	MLB	34	0.65	1.06	3.08	0.9	97.5	59.6	15.1	49.9
2018	HOU	MLB	35	0.90	2.52	2.33	7.3	97.5	61.2	16.2	51.6
2019	HOU	MLB	36	0.80	2.58	2.51	7.9	96.8	49.9	17.5	48.3
2020	HOU	MLB	37	1.01	2.75	2.95	5.3	95.8	54.6	15.1	48.2

Pitchers

Let's give our pitchers a turn, using 2019 AL Cy Young winner Justin Verlander as our example. Take a look at his stat block: the first line and the **YEAR**, **TEAM**, **LVL** and **AGE** columns are the same as in the position player example earlier.

Here too, we have a series of columns that display raw, unadjusted statistics compiled by the pitcher over the course of a season: **W** (wins), **L** (losses), **SV** (saves), **G** (games pitched), **GS** (games started), **IP** (innings pitched), **H** (hits allowed) and **HR** (home runs allowed). Next we have two statistics that are rates: **BB/9** (walks per nine innings) and **K/9** (strikeouts per nine innings), before returning to the unadjusted K (strikeouts).

Next up is **GB%** (ground ball percentage), which is the percentage of all batted balls that were hit on the ground, including both outs and hits. Remember, this is based on observational data and subject to human error, so please approach this with a healthy dose of skepticism.

BABIP (batting average on balls in play) is calculated using the same methodology as it is for position players, but it often tells us more about a pitcher than it does a hitter. With pitchers, a high BABIP is often due to poor defense or bad luck, and can often be an indicator of potential rebound, and a low BABIP may be cause to expect performance regression. (A typical league-average BABIP is close to .290-.300.)

The metrics **WHIP** (walks plus hits per inning pitched) and **ERA** (earned run average) are old standbys: WHIP measures walks and hits allowed on a per-inning basis, while ERA measures earned runs on a nine-inning basis. Neither of these stats are translated or adjusted.

DRA (Deserved Run Average) was described at length earlier, and measures how many runs the pitcher "deserved" to allow per nine innings. Please note that since we lack all the data points that would make for a "real" DRA for minor-league events, the DRA displayed for minor league partial-seasons is based off of different data. (That data is a modified version of our cFIP metric, which you can find more information about on our website.)

Just like with hitters, **WARP** (Wins Above Replacement Player) is a total value metric that puts pitchers of all stripes on the same scale as position players. We use DRA as the primary input for our calculation of WARP. You might notice that relief pitchers (due to their limited innings) may have a lower WARP than you were expecting or than you might see in other WARP-like metrics. WARP does not take leverage into account, just the actions a pitcher performs and the expected value of those actions...which ends up judging high-leverage relief pitchers differently than you might imagine given their prestige and market value.

MPH gives you the pitcher's 95th percentile velocity for the noted season, in order to give you an idea of what the *peak* fastball velocity a pitcher possesses. Since this comes from our pitch-tracking data, it is not publicly available for minor-league pitchers.

Finally, we display the three new pitching metrics we described earlier. **FB%** (fastball percentage) gives you the percentage of fastballs thrown out of all pitches. **WHF** (whiff rate) tells you the percentage of swinging strikes induced out of all pitches. **CSP** (called strike probability) expresses the likelihood of all pitches thrown to result in a called strike, after controlling for factors like handedness, umpire, pitch type, count and location.

PECOTA

All players have PECOTA projections for 2020, as well as a set of other numbers that describe the performance of comparable players according to PECOTA. All projections for 2020 are for the player at the date we went to press in early January and are projected into the league and park context as indicated by the team abbreviation. (Note that players at very low levels of the minors are too unpredictable to assess using these numbers.) All PECOTA projected statistics represent a player's projected major-league performance.

Below the projections are the player's three highest-scoring comparable players as determined by PECOTA. All comparables represent a snapshot of how the listed player was performing at the same age as the current player, so if a

23-year-old pitcher is compared to Bartolo Colón, he's actually being compared to a 23-year-old Colón, not the version that pitched for the Rangers in 2018, nor to Colón's career as a whole.

A few points about pitcher projections. First, we aren't yet projecting peak velocity, so that column will be blank in the PECOTA lines. Second, projecting DRA is trickier than evaluating past performance, because it is unclear how deserving each pitcher will be of his anticipated outcomes. However, we know that another DRA-related statistic–contextual FIP or cFIP-estimates future run scoring very well. So for PECOTA, the projected DRA figures you see are based on the past cFIPs generated by the pitcher and comparable players over time, along with the other factors described above.

Lineouts

In each chapter's Lineouts section, you'll find abbreviated text comments, as well as all the same information you'd find in our full player comments. The only difference is that we limit the stats boxes in this section to only including the 2019 information for each player.

Managers

After all those wonderful team chapters, we've got statistics for each big-league manager, all of whom are organized by alphabetical order. Here you'll find a block including an extraordinary amount of information collected from each manager's entire career. For more information on the acronyms and what they mean, please visit the Glossary at www.baseballprospectus.com.

There is one important metric that we'd like to call attention to, and you'll find it next to each manager's name: **wRM+** (weighted reliever management plus). Developed by Rob Arthur and Rian Watt, wRM+ investigates how good a manager is at using their best relievers during the moments of highest leverage, using both our proprietary DRA metric as well as Leverage Index. wRM+ is scaled to a league average of 100, and a wRM+ of 105 indicates that relievers were used approximately five percent "better" than average. On the other hand, a wRM+ of 95 would tell us the team used its relievers five percent "worse" than the average team.

While wRM+ does not have an extremely strong correlation with a manager, it is statistically significant; this means that a manager is not *entirely* responsible for a team's wRM+, but does have some effect on that number.

PECOTA Leaderboards

If you're familiar with PECOTA, then you'll have noticed that the projection system often appears bullish on players coming off a bad year and bearish on players coming off a good year. (This is because the system weights several previous seasons, not just the most recent one.) In addition, we publish the 50th

Oakland Athletics 2020

percentile projections for each player–which is smack in the middle of the range of projected production—which tends to mean PECOTA stat lines don't often have extreme results like 40 home runs or 250 strikeouts in a given season. In essence, PECOTA doesn't project very many extreme seasons.

At the end of the book, we've ranked the top players at each position based on their PECOTA projections. This might help you visualize just how a given player's projection compares to that of their peers, so that even if a dramatic stat line isn't projected, you can still imagine how they stack up against the rest of the league.

Part 1: Team Analysis

Oakland A's: Where Are You Going, Where Have You Been?

Craig Brown, Wilson Karaman and Matthew Trueblood

2019: What Went Right

The A's had what can only be described as a Very Oakland Year, which, to be clear, is a positive thing. It was almost a carbon-copy season from the year before where they started slow and went on a tear beginning in mid-June. On June 16, the A's held a 37-36 record and were in third place in the AL West. From that point on they surged to a 60-29 record and another 97-win season. Who can argue against 97 wins, a run differential of +165 and a spot in the Wild Card Game? Final result be damned.

The offense was powered primarily by players Oakland obtained in the draft or via trade (read: they ain't signing free agents). And powered it was. The A's hit 257 dingers, the most in club history. It was the eighth-highest single-season total in major-league history, yet only good enough to rank fifth in 2019. A franchise-record seven players hit 20 or more home runs.

The offense averaged 5.2 runs per game and was led by shortstop Marcus Semien, who enjoyed an absolutely transformative, breakout season, an offensive tour de force and an all-out assault on the Oakland record books. With 7.5 WARP, he had the third-best season in the AL behind a couple of guys named Trout and Bregman. He scored 123 runs, tying the Oakland franchise record (Reggie Jackson, 1969 edition) and finished third on the club single-season lists with 83 extra base hits, 187 hits, and 343 total bases.

And then there was Semien's defense. When he arrived in the East Bay in 2015, his defensive reputation was odiferous. That year he ranked 53rd out of 58 shortstops on our FRAA leaderboard at -4.4. This season, his turnaround was complete: He finished with a 4.2 FRAA, the 11th-best out of 59 shortstops. He finished a deserved third in the MVP balloting.

Speaking of well-rounded play, Matt Chapman did it all once again for Oakland. Completing his third season in the majors, he is the top third baseman in the league according to FRAA (12.9) and finished with a 120 DRC+. He hit a career-high 36 home runs. Matt Olson also had a career-high 36 dingers despite missing 34 games after suffering an injury in the season-opening series in Japan. He didn't miss a beat when he came back, playing second fiddle on the team with an average exit velocity of 91.9 mph to Chapman's 92.6 mph.

Mark Canha and Ramón Laureano were both members of the aforementioned 20-homer club. If Canha got the ball in the air, look out. He finished with a 21 percent HR/FB rate. Laureano hit in the lower third of the order for the first two months of the season. Once he moved up in the lineup in mid-June, he hit 331/.390/.663 the rest of the way, with 14 of his 24 home runs—this despite missing 32 games to the IL. Given that all of the above players were either signed or acquired via trade, the lethal Oakland offense can only be described as a scouting and developmental success.

On the pitching side, Executive VP of Baseball Operations Billy Beane and General Manager David Forst splashed some cash on the free agent market in the offseason. Mike Fiers, acquired during the now-defunct waiver trading period in August of 2018, was retained at a cost of two years and $14.1 million. He rewarded the A's with 33 starts, a 3.90 ERA and 5.06 DRA. Oft-injured Brett Anderson was brought back with moderate expectations at $1.5 million, yet tied a career-high with 31 starts and 176 innings. A bit of a throwback with a 4.6 SO/9, he nevertheless finished with a 3.89 ERA and a 5.65 DRA. The advanced metrics of the A's top starting pitching duo isn't impressive at all, yet the team won 42 of their combined 64 starts, a .656 winning percentage.

Chris Bassitt reached career highs in starts and innings pitched on his way to an 8.8 SO/9 and 2.9 BB/9. He finished with a 3.81 ERA and 4.45 DRA, good for a 2.0 WARP. He ran out of steam toward the end of the season before the A's shifted him to the bullpen. They also got a healthy Sean Manaea back at the end of the season and, when combined with Jesus Luzardo and A.J. Puk, gave the A's a look at what potential top of the rotation arms look like. Health permitting, next year looks like a good one for the rotation.

2019: What Went Wrong

I am contractually obligated to drop at least one Moneyball reference in any Oakland A's season recap so here goes: In the book, Beane famously said, "My shit doesn't work in the playoffs. My job is to get us to the playoffs. What happens after that is fucking luck." We need to amend this quote from playoffs to simply the Wild Card. Since the league went to a one-game, win-or-go-home Wild Card matchup to advance to the Divisional Series in 2012, the Yankees and A's both have had the most appearances in this game with three apiece (the Pirates have also had three appearances on the NL side). The Yankees have won two of those games. The A's are 0-3. In fact, their losing streak in deciding postseason games has now stretched to nine, the worst mark in MLB history. Oakland's October record this millennium is the stuff of nightmares:

2000 ALDS lost 3-2
2001 ALDS lost 3-2
2002 ALDS lost 3-2
2003 ALDS lost 3-2
2006 ALDS won 3-0
2006 ALCS lost 4-0
2012 ALDS lost 3-2
2013 ALDS lost 3-2
2014 ALWC lost
2018 ALWC lost
2019 ALWC lost

This is the appropriate place to mention how Khris Davis let everyone down in 2019. The world is quite literally on fire. We crave the familiar, the comfortable. Davis and his .247 batting average is the baseball version of chicken pot pie. It's not exactly the best thing going, but who cares? It's fun, reliable and tasty. After finishing at .247 for four consecutive years, Davis could only muster .220 in what was his worst offensive season since he arrived in the bigs in 2013. His DRC+ of 91, .293 OBP, and .387 slugging percentages were also the worst marks of his career. The dip in power was especially troubling considering he's on the wrong side of 30. He managed just 34 extra-base hits and saw his ISO drop to .166, nearly 90 points below his career mark. The silver arbitrary endpoint was that on May 21 Davis was hitting .247 when he hit the IL with a left hip contusion. He wasn't the same after the injury and hit .207 the rest of the way once he returned. Nothing lasts forever.

Frankie Montas was in the midst of a breakout season in the rotation before he was dinged with an 80-game suspension for testing positive for Ostarin, a performance-enhancing drug. He returned for one final start in September but was ineligible for the postseason. Montas finished with a 3.16 DRA, 2.7 WARP, and the odor of regret.

It's a long season, and the A's started it in Japan, so you are forgiven if you don't recall the Kendrys Morales Era. When Olson went on the IL after undergoing a hamate excision procedure after that season-opening series, Oakland, desperate for a 1B/DH type, surfed the waiver wire and came upon Morales, who had just been designated by Toronto. At least the A's only covered around $2 million of the $12 million owed to the aging slugger. Olson recovered enough to play in 127 games. Meanwhile, Morales bombed out, hitting just a single home run while seeing his ISO crater to .056 in the East Bay, nearly 140 points below his career average. He was released in May. —*Craig Brown*

Prospect Outlook

It's a lovely time to be alive and an Oakland Athletic, at least on non-win-or-go-home game days. Oakland's young are on the wax right now, with a stout system shadowing a very good young core at the big-league level. Luzardo and A.J. Puk are good bets to contribute dominant major-league innings next year; the two represent the most electric ready-for-The-Show tandem of arms in baseball.

We got a fine accounting of the duo's batterymate, **Sean Murphy**, for the next several years down the stretch as well, and in a limited sample he did what he can and probably will do. Perhaps most excitingly of all, there are some very A's pitching prospects bubbling up into likely relevance for next season in the hot quartet of **Daulton Jefferies**, **Parker Dunshee**, **James Kaprielian**, and **Grant Holmes**. The formers are stuff-limited out-getters in fine Oakland form, while the latter are "maybe!" stuff-and injury-havers. —*Wilson Karaman*

2020 Outlook

The Jurickson Profar experiment didn't work out at all in Oakland, though he hit into some bad luck and looked absolutely ravishing in the team's many uniforms. (Then again, who doesn't?) With the Padres looking to remake their infield, the A's pounced on an opportunity to add quality depth both at catcher (where Austin Allen should be the backup come Opening Day) and in the outfield (where Buddy Reed offers medium-term upside and doesn't need to be added to the 40-man roster until December). Forst also re-signed Jake Diekman, whom the team acquired for bullpen help in July, and whose slider-driven strikeout skills make him a solid middle reliever for a team that leans as heavily on its relief corps as anyone. Tony Kemp came very cheaply, in a January trade with the Cubs, and can replace what Profar gave them as a part-time second baseman—though not, of course, what they'd hoped Profar would give them.

Beyond that, it was a typically quiet winter for the A's. They only shake things up when they anticipate moving into or out of a new phase, and right now, they're clearly smack-dab in the middle of a window. As long as Chapman and Olson are anchoring the infield, they keep finding surprising late-bloomers, and their pitching remains young and inexpensive, they're a threat, but they have self-imposed restraints that prevent them from getting deeper into October. One more star, almost anywhere on the roster, would shake things up and make them AL West favorites, but they always stop at one move short. —*Matthew Trueblood*

Performance Graphs

2019 Hit List Ranking

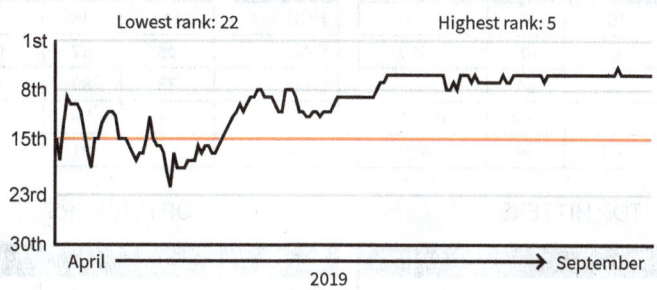

Committed Payroll (in millions)

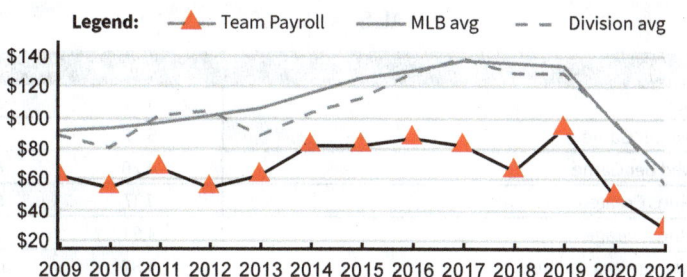

Farm System Ranking

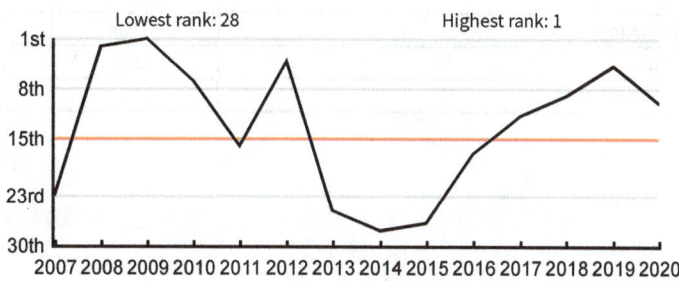

2019 Team Performance

ACTUAL STANDINGS

Team	W	L	Pct
HOU	107	55	0.660
OAK	**97**	**65**	**0.599**
TEX	78	84	0.481
LAA	72	90	0.444
SEA	68	94	0.420

THIRD-ORDER STANDINGS

Team	W	L	Pct
HOU	117	45	0.719
OAK	**95**	**67**	**0.584**
LAA	73	89	0.453
SEA	72	90	0.444
TEX	71	91	0.437

TOP HITTERS

Player	WARP
Marcus Semien	7.5
Matt Chapman	5.2
Ramón Laureano	4.2

TOP PITCHERS

Player	WARP
Frankie Montas	2.7
Liam Hendriks	2.4
Chris Bassitt	2.0

VITAL STATISTICS

Statistic Name	Value	Rank
Pythagenpat	.602	5th
Runs Scored per Game	5.22	8th
Runs Allowed per Game	4.20	6th
Deserved Runs Created Plus	107	5th
Deserved Run Average	4.91	15th
Fielding Independent Pitching	4.37	15th
Defensive Efficiency Rating	.722	3rd
Batter Age	27.8	12th
Pitcher Age	30.6	28th
Salary	$92.7M	25th
Marginal $ per Marginal Win	$1.6M	29th
Injured List Days	1225	22nd
$ on IL	13%	10th

2020 Team Projections

PROJECTED STANDINGS

Team	W	L	Pct	+/-
HOU	98.3	63.7	0.607	-9
LAA	86.8	75.2	0.536	15
OAK	84.6	77.4	0.522	-12
TEX	73.0	89.0	0.451	-5
SEA	66.0	96.0	0.407	-2

TOP PROJECTED HITTERS

Player	WARP
Matt Chapman	4.2
Marcus Semien	4.1
Ramón Laureano	3.5

TOP PROJECTED PITCHERS

Player	WARP
Jesus Luzardo	1.6
Sean Manaea	1.5
Liam Hendriks	1.5

FARM SYSTEM REPORT

Top Prospect	Number of Top 101 Prospects
Jesus Luzardo, #9	3

KEY DEDUCTIONS

Player	WARP
Tanner Roark	1.2
Blake Treinen	0.6
Jharel Cotton	0.5
Brett Anderson	0.5
Homer Bailey	0.4
Jurickson Profar	0.2
Josh Phegley	-0.5

KEY ADDITIONS

Player	WARP
Austin Allen	0.8
Vimael Machin	0.4
Jonah Heim	0.3
Parker Dunshee	0.1
Tony Kemp	0.0
T.J. McFarland	-0.1
Daulton Jefferies	-0.1
Burch Smith	-0.1

Team Personnel

Executive Vice President of Baseball Operations
Billy Beane

General Manager
David Forst

Assistant General Manager, Major League and International Operations
Dan Feinstein

Assistant General Manager/Director of Player Personnel
Billy Owens

Manager
Bob Melvin

Oakland-Alameda County Coliseum Stats

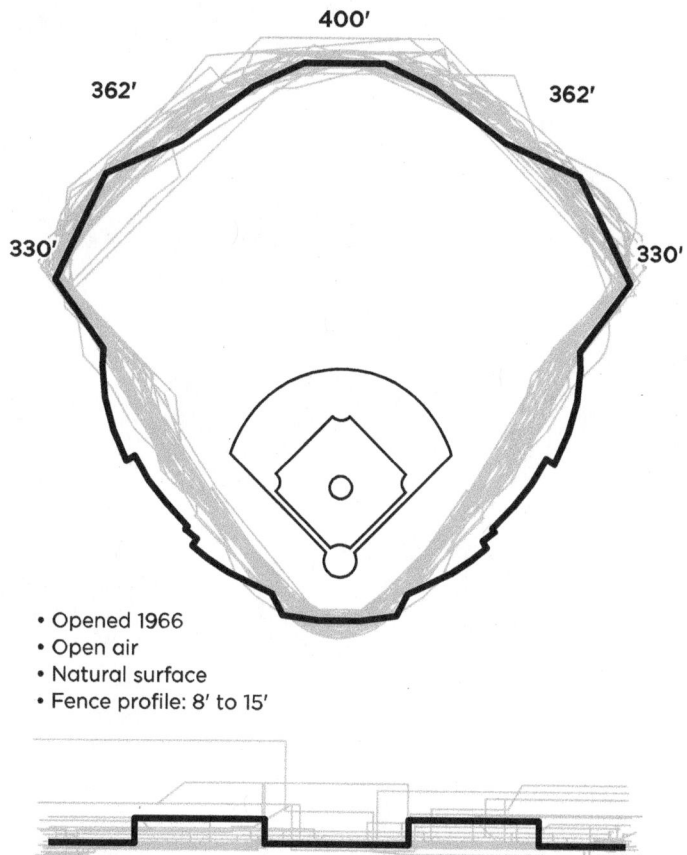

- Opened 1966
- Open air
- Natural surface
- Fence profile: 8' to 15'

Three-Year Park Factors

Runs	Runs/RH	Runs/LH	HR/RH	HR/LH
98	100	94	96	93

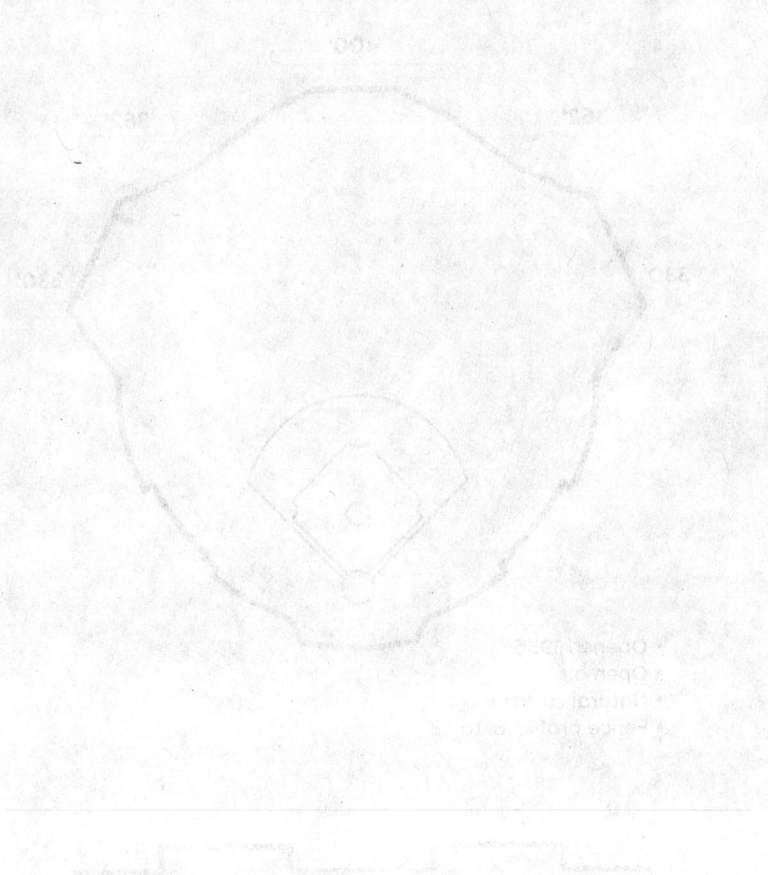

Athletics Team Analysis

One of the more offbeat plays of the 2019 season happened on a Thursday afternoon in Kansas City, on August 29th. The Oakland A's held an 8-7 lead in the top of the ninth with runners on second and third when Royals third baseman Cheslor Cuthbert chased a pop-up into foul territory, making a leaning catch on the top step of the visitor's dugout before momentum carried him the rest of the way down.

It was a good catch and a bad play. The batter, Corban Joseph, was retired on the foul out, but umpire Chris Segal, either anticipating confusion or just generally emphatic as umpires are, vigorously motioned for the runner on third to score. Cuthbert stopped dead in his tracks; Seth Brown trotted home and was received with noncommittal high fives.

The rule behind this sequence of events, 5.06(b)(3)(C), states: "If a fielder, after having made a legal catch, should step or fall into any out-of-play area, the ball is dead and each runner shall advance one base, without liability to be put out, from his last legally touched base at the time the fielder entered such out-of-play area." The A's got an insurance run out of the deal, and they needed it, since the Royals later scored what would have been the tying run in the bottom of the ninth.

It's important that this game happened in Kansas City. Had it been played in Oakland, Cuthbert might have gone the rest of his career unaware of Rule 5.06(b)(3)(C). He might have made the equivalent catch fully upright with several steps to go before meeting the dugout, thanks to the Oakland Coliseum's generous foul territory.

Happily tangled in the spirit of the game is the romantic notion, unique to baseball among sports, that architecture can and should wield influence. You can see it at field level in Fenway's Green Monster, Yankee Stadium's short porch, the catwalks and white roof at The Trop, and Oakland's foul ground. While Major League Baseball's rule book is firm on the sacred 90-foot sides of the diamond, it offers only rough suggestions when it comes to perimeter dimensions and miscellaneous park quirks. It follows that architecture also impacts baseball on a tactical level, as coaches and front office staff must decide which players' skills are a match for their own confines or potentially disastrous in those they encounter on the road.

Oakland Athletics 2020

The win at Kauffman Stadium was one of 97 on the year, and it looms significant—as all unlikely wins tend to—given the single-game margin that kept the A's above the Tampa Bay Rays in the final American League Wild Card standings. Over 54,000 fans gathered in the Coliseum for the play-in game, setting a major-league record for Wild Card game attendance. They even spilled over into Mount Davis, that aftermarket eye-sore that wooed the Raiders back to town in 1995, obscured a wide view of the Oakland hills, and now remains mostly tarped in the name of "intimacy," a softer quality invoked because it's more appealing than "artificial scarcity."

This night held all the conditions for home-field advantage when it's been relentlessly hammered home what a disadvantage the Coliseum is and how shaky the team's presence in Oakland is as a result. Plans, renderings, stalled talks, and even lawsuits surrounding the pursuit of a new stadium landed as syncopated drum beats throughout the season. Although the A's lost their third Wild Card game that evening, the atmosphere was devout and defiant, a realization of the building's original premise with acknowledgment of all it's been through along the way.

The Oakland–Alameda County Coliseum complex was completed in 1966, garnering praise for its elegant geometry and sensible, multi-sport functionality. Its raw concrete exterior was an extension of the earnest post-war spirit of renewal seen in other Brutalist buildings of the era. You can watch old black and white news footage of a local reporter comparing it to the Roman Colosseum "if you look quickly as you drive by it," a load-bearing caveat that does nothing to detract from the apparent optimism.

Equally relevant to the design, concrete was cheap. Publicly financed for $25 million (still a bargain at roughly $213 million in today's dollars), the complex comprising both the Coliseum and the adjacent arena was designed by Myron Goldsmith from Skidmore, Owings & Merrill, the firm responsible for skyscrapers including the Willis Tower (previously Sears Tower) in Chicago, One World Trade Center in New York, and the Burj Khalifa in Dubai, currently the tallest structure in the world.

The Coliseum was designed with a modest profile, sunken into the earth below grade, literally rooted in Oakland, if you will. Just over 50 years later, with the Coliseum as the last remaining "concrete doughnut" replete with unpredictable plumbing, sparse attendance, and an unknown number of resident possums, the A's have had to find new ways to embrace that grounded quality and draw on the community they're nestled in.

One of the main elements distinguishing architecture from fine art is function. A structure can't simply be beautiful; it must be engineered and designed for practical use. In changing the prescribed function, you also change the criteria by which the structure is assessed. An office building does not make for a good church sanctuary, no matter how ardently capitalism tries to convince us otherwise.

By 2019, the A's had replaced traditional season ticket plans with "A's Access" membership, a natural fit for a team with seats to spare and an audience accustomed to subscription models. For a reasonable price, benefits include general admission to all home games plus discounts on concessions and merchandise. Where the Coliseum lacked the bevy of dining options surrounding other urban stadiums, the A's invited local food trucks to be part of "Championship Plaza," a pre-game gathering spot just outside the park.

All of this, coupled with the everyday nature of baseball's schedule, made it possible and desirable to spend a lot more time at the ballpark. In this way, the A's altered the Coliseum's function; by making the game-going experience something less lofty and precious, they relaxed the standards one might otherwise apply to the built environment. This is to say: it's harder to complain when you've paid $7 for a hot dog and beer, get to watch a 97-win team, and will be back later in the week (if not the very next day).

"The Coliseum is baseball's last dive bar," wrote Jack Nicas in a *New York Times* essay. Neighborhood bars, along with rec centers, places of worship, and barbershops, are common examples of what the urban sociologist Ray Oldenburg termed the "third place": "a setting beyond home and work (the 'first' and 'second' places, respectively) in which people relax in good company and do so on a regular basis." As a widely-accessible home away from home, why not add the Coliseum to that list?

These informal meeting places, Oldenburg argues, are essential for building community and even for maintaining the grass roots of democracy. Anchored by central figures the urbanist Jane Jacobs called "public characters" (e.g. the outfield bleacher regulars with their drums, banners, and bells), people of different backgrounds can share in a common purpose and cultivate a sense of ownership. In this environment it's easy to become fiercely protective of the Coliseum, to love the humble surroundings and wear them as a badge of pride. "I like that it's not glamorized," Khris Davis told the *San Francisco Chronicle's* John Shea in 2016. "You've got to change your attitude, you've got to come with the right attitude here every day to perform."

It's especially easy to feel this way when the team is playing well. Despite the Coliseum's reputation as a pitcher's park, seven Athletics hit 20 or more home runs in 2019: Matt Olson, Matt Chapman, Marcus Semien, Mark Canha, Ramón Laureano, Davis, and Jurickson Profar. Olson and Chapman won Gold Gloves as part of an indispensable defense. Semien had a banner year with 7.5 WARP and finished third in AL MVP voting. All-Star Liam Hendriks offered late-inning security with a 1.80 ERA, and Jesus Luzardo was a crystalline vision of the future in a handful of electric appearances.

But in worse times, say, in the immediate aftermath of a Wild Card loss, the Coliseum seems like an emblem of this franchise's inability to break into the league's upper tier, if not partly the cause of it. Architecture's influence is not only physical and tactical but emotional. Baseball is a game played and watched by humans, and it's difficult to feel like a first-rate club when the ceiling is leaking, when your surroundings feel fragile, irrelevant or impermanent.

In *The Architecture of Happiness*, Alain de Botton writes, "Belief in the significance of architecture is premised on the notion that we are, for better or for worse, different people in different places—and on the conviction that it is architecture's task to render vivid to us who we might ideally be."

First shared in November 2018 and since modified according to public feedback, renderings of the A's proposed waterfront park at Howard Terminal are boldly contemporary, fitting for a franchise that has always identified as audacious and a bit different. Designed by Bjarke Ingels Group, the plans are a welcome departure from the now-ubiquitous "retro" stadiums, some of which paired red brick and steel with so many custom amenities and motifs that they ironically appear postmodern rather than classic.

It's an open design, playing foil to the Coliseum's walled fortress, and its airiness also symbolizes what architecture critic Paul Goldberger observes as "the current trend of extending a team's sphere of influence out beyond the ballpark gates and of trying to create a new neighborhood in which the ballpark can sit." To that end, the plans include surrounding high-rises and other businesses. "Bigger than baseball," is how the team described it.

All of this is nice enough, but is it really the design itself, the cosmetic upgrades and touted features like an elevated rooftop park that has stoked fans' desires? Or is it powerful because it grants permission to dream of deep playoff runs, contract extensions and free agent signings; a vision of the actualized self, as de Botton describes?

It's both, and it's more. Architecture's final realm of influence is financial, particularly so when it comes to sports stadiums. Without a good dose of luck, the A's actually can't succeed without the revenue a new stadium brings. This became a pressing concern when the CBA introduced a schedule of revenue sharing restrictions for the team in 2016, and in 2020, the A's will be fully disqualified from revenue sharing. Anticipated contract extensions wait in the wings.

The prolific Bay Area architect and teacher William Wurster saw architecture as "the picture frame, not the picture." With top prospects ready to hit the majors next season and a foundation of home-grown talent already soaring, the "picture" for the Oakland Athletics is fine indeed, though it longs for some gilding around the edges.

—*Clarissa Young is a former author of Baseball Prospectus.*

Part 2: Player Analysis

Oakland Athletics 2020

PLAYER COMMENTS WITH GRAPHS

Franklin Barreto 2B
Born: 02/27/96 Age: 24 Bats: R Throws: R
Height: 5'10" Weight: 200 Origin: International Free Agent, 2012

YEAR	TEAM	LVL	AGE	PA	R	2B	3B	HR	RBI	BB	K	SB	CS	AVG/OBP/SLG
2017	NAS	AAA	21	510	63	19	7	15	54	27	141	15	8	.290/.339/.456
2017	OAK	MLB	21	76	10	1	2	2	6	5	33	2	0	.197/.250/.352
2018	NAS	AAA	22	333	54	16	1	18	46	39	106	5	2	.259/.357/.514
2018	OAK	MLB	22	75	10	4	0	5	16	1	29	0	0	.233/.253/.493
2019	LVG	AAA	23	424	88	29	5	19	65	42	113	15	1	.295/.374/.552
2019	OAK	MLB	23	58	6	2	0	2	5	1	23	1	0	.123/.138/.263
2020	OAK	MLB	24	455	46	20	2	14	52	30	149	10	4	.220/.281/.383

Comparables: Javier Báez, Adalberto Mondesi, Roy McMillan

It seems an age since the A's shipped Josh Donaldson to Toronto for a package headlined by Baretto and Brett Lawrie. Normally, we could toss on another sentence about how sad it is to see a young buck's career come to this and move on to the next blurb, but this is supposed to be about Barreto. Even though he's been in the public consciousness for five years, he's still just 24, and he's never really had an extended audition at the highest level. You'd rather be a top prospect than a post-hype sleeper, but the tools seem mostly intact and Barreto's career still has a pulse. He does himself no favors with auditions like he gave in Oakland last summer, but he needs to get a few months of sustained playing time before we can write him off entirely.

YEAR	TEAM	LVL	AGE	PA	DRC+	VORP	BABIP	BRR	FRAA	WARP
2017	NAS	AAA	21	510	104	34.7	.384	0.3	SS(83): -3.3, 2B(25): -2.6	1.9
2017	OAK	MLB	21	76	55	0.4	.333	0.7	SS(11): 0.3, 2B(10): 0.2	0.0
2018	NAS	AAA	22	333	127	35.6	.337	3.5	2B(60): -2.2, SS(11): 0.4	2.3
2018	OAK	MLB	22	75	76	-0.8	.308	-1.1	2B(26): -1.7, SS(2): 0.0	-0.3
2019	LVG	AAA	23	424	108	31.7	.374	2.2	2B(47): -5.1, SS(30): 0.1	1.8
2019	OAK	MLB	23	58	50	-1.6	.156	0.5	2B(17): -0.2, SS(5): -0.2	-0.1
2020	OAK	MLB	24	455	75	2.7	.304	-0.5	2B -5, SS 0	-0.2

Franklin Barreto, continued

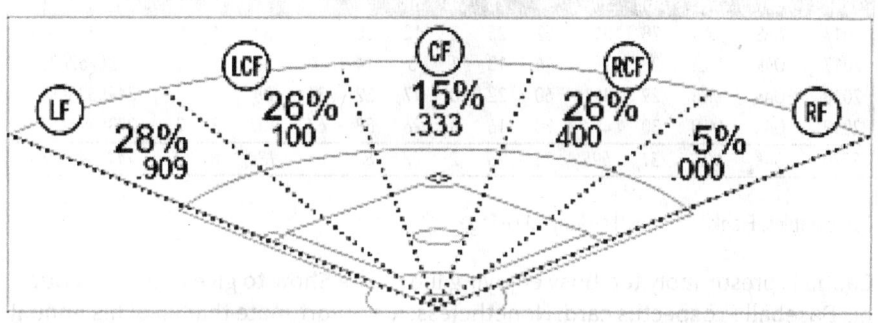

Batted Ball Distribution

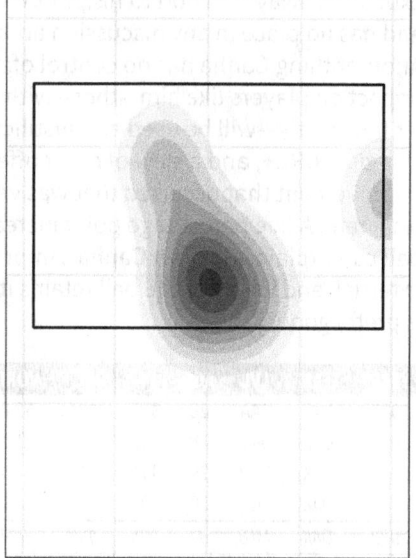

Oakland Athletics 2020

Mark Canha OF

Born: 02/15/89   Age: 31   Bats: R   Throws: R
Height: 6'2"   Weight: 212   Origin: Round 7, 2010 Draft (#227 overall)

YEAR	TEAM	LVL	AGE	PA	R	2B	3B	HR	RBI	BB	K	SB	CS	AVG/OBP/SLG
2017	NAS	AAA	28	317	52	25	3	12	50	34	62	4	0	.283/.373/.529
2017	OAK	MLB	28	187	16	13	1	5	14	7	56	2	0	.208/.262/.382
2018	OAK	MLB	29	411	60	22	0	17	52	34	88	1	2	.249/.328/.449
2019	OAK	MLB	30	497	80	16	3	26	58	67	107	3	2	.273/.396/.517
2020	OAK	MLB	31	595	76	25	2	27	83	61	138	6	2	.244/.343/.460

Comparables: Franklin Stubbs, Lee May, Mike Laga

Canha is presumably too busy enjoying life in The Show to give two rips about his Baseball Prospectus card. Nonetheless, it's unfortunate that all of his Annual comments reference the occasion Oakland took him in the Rule 5 draft, as that legacy seemingly defines every twist and turn in his career. Each milestone is thus a surprise (he was a Rule 5 guy once, you know!) and each setback explained away by a nod to his prior fungibility. It all feels reductive and unfair, and has no place in any discussion about his 3.5 WARP breakout 2019 season. Another thing Canha has no control of: the ball. Its disproportionately positive impact on players like him—those with middling power who put the ball in the air frequently—will be used as a justification for his career-high in home runs, slugging, DRC+, and a slew of other offensive categories. It belies an improvement that occurred that was very much in Canha's control, though: his walk rate. A five percentage point increased established a career high. A livelier ball can explain a lot, but Canha's improvement was as much internal as it was external, and whether the ball retains its 2019 traits or not, Canha's new normal is pretty good.

YEAR	TEAM	LVL	AGE	PA	DRC+	VORP	BABIP	BRR	FRAA	WARP
2017	NAS	AAA	28	317	136	33.0	.323	3.3	RF(61): -2.7, CF(8): 0.9	2.3
2017	OAK	MLB	28	187	67	-2.8	.274	0.3	RF(22): -1.0, LF(20): -0.9	-0.6
2018	OAK	MLB	29	411	115	18.8	.282	-0.3	CF(62): -5.9, LF(51): 1.4	1.5
2019	OAK	MLB	30	497	135	36.9	.308	1.3	CF(56): -3.8, RF(27): 1.9	3.5
2020	OAK	MLB	31	595	113	26.4	.282	0.8	LF 7, CF -1	3.1

Mark Canha, continued

Batted Ball Distribution

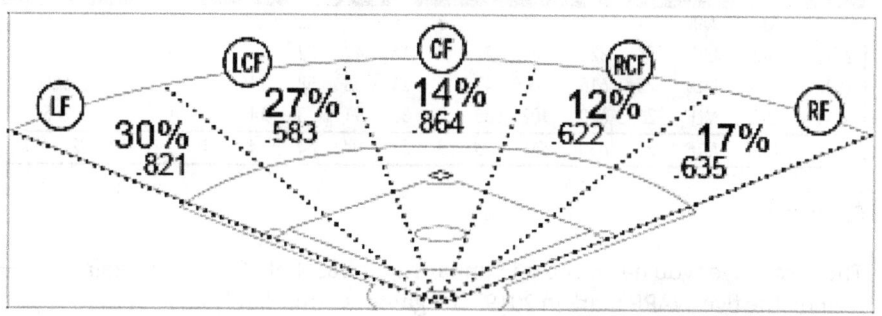

Strike Zone vs LHP   Strike Zone vs RHP

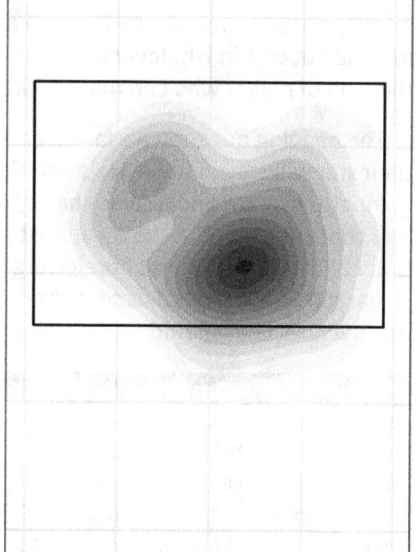

Matt Chapman 3B

Born: 04/28/93 Age: 27 Bats: R Throws: R
Height: 6'0" Weight: 220 Origin: Round 1, 2014 Draft (#25 overall)

YEAR	TEAM	LVL	AGE	PA	R	2B	3B	HR	RBI	BB	K	SB	CS	AVG/OBP/SLG
2017	NAS	AAA	24	204	30	6	2	16	30	25	63	5	4	.257/.348/.589
2017	OAK	MLB	24	326	39	23	2	14	40	32	92	0	3	.234/.313/.472
2018	OAK	MLB	25	616	100	42	6	24	68	58	146	1	2	.278/.356/.508
2019	OAK	MLB	26	670	102	36	3	36	91	73	147	1	1	.249/.342/.506
2020	OAK	MLB	27	630	80	33	3	33	94	64	146	4	2	.235/.321/.481

Comparables: Pedro Álvarez, Jake Lamb, Troy Glaus

The best player you never see on Sunday Night Baseball, Chapman again topped the five-WARP mark in 2019. The game is remarkably flush in third basemen these days, and while it's easy to lose a good one in the shuffle, it shouldn't be Chapman. At the plate, he's a formidable hitter, and he pressed through a July swoon to notch his second straight season of a 120 DRC+ or better. Defensively, he's developed a signature all to his own, stretching out into an exaggerated, wide-legged crouch as the pitch comes in and efficiently leaping out of it in whatever direction the ball travels. He's a star, full stop, and the kind of player who can make a kid really *want* to play baseball.

The nagging question A's fans won't want to consider is how much longer their star will stay in town. He's entering his third full season, and with a competitive team and a salary barely over the minimum, he's not going anywhere in 2020. But the A's almost religiously make a habit of observing Branch Rickey's wisdom of preferring to trade a man a year too early rather than a year too late; there's a decent chance Chapman's Oakland career is more than half over. A's fans should enjoy their man while they can.

YEAR	TEAM	LVL	AGE	PA	DRC+	VORP	BABIP	BRR	FRAA	WARP
2017	NAS	AAA	24	204	130	20.8	.293	-0.1	3B(49): 7.2	2.2
2017	OAK	MLB	24	326	97	14.9	.290	-1.0	3B(84): 12.6	2.2
2018	OAK	MLB	25	616	125	47.9	.338	3.8	3B(145): 15.6	6.2
2019	OAK	MLB	26	670	120	43.8	.270	-3.2	3B(156): 12.9	5.2
2020	OAK	MLB	27	630	108	22.3	.259	0.4	3B 17	4.1

Matt Chapman, continued

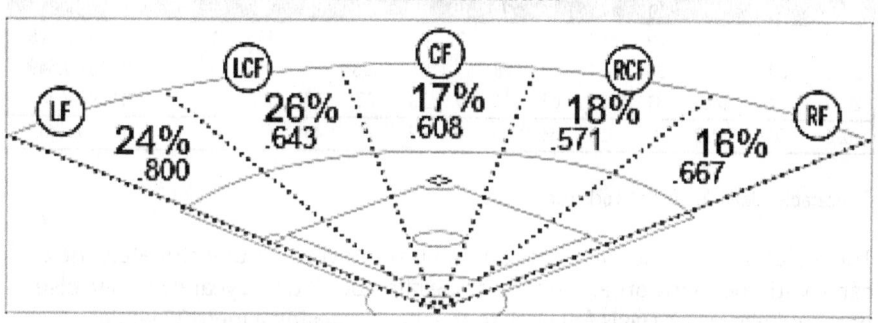

Batted Ball Distribution

Strike Zone vs LHP   **Strike Zone vs RHP**

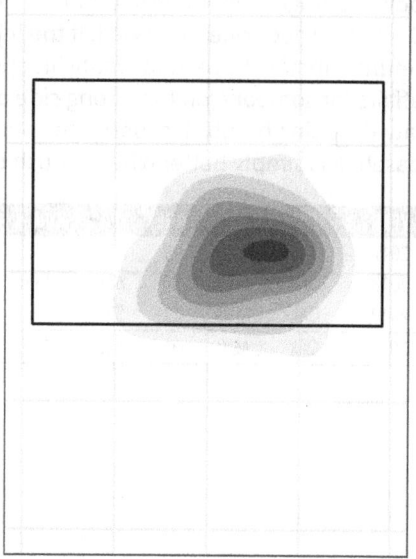

Oakland Athletics 2020

Khris Davis LF

Born: 12/21/87 Age: 32 Bats: R Throws: R
Height: 5'11" Weight: 203 Origin: Round 7, 2009 Draft (#226 overall)

YEAR	TEAM	LVL	AGE	PA	R	2B	3B	HR	RBI	BB	K	SB	CS	AVG/OBP/SLG
2017	OAK	MLB	29	652	91	28	1	43	110	73	195	4	0	.247/.336/.528
2018	OAK	MLB	30	654	98	28	1	48	123	59	175	0	0	.247/.326/.549
2019	OAK	MLB	31	533	61	11	0	23	73	47	146	0	0	.220/.293/.387
2020	OAK	MLB	32	525	66	20	1	29	78	46	151	3	1	.230/.306/.457

Comparables: Matt Joyce, Don Lock, Lucas Duda

The run of .247 batting averages couldn't last forever, and unfortunately the end came with too many other red flags to be glib about it. In a year everyone else homered like crazy, Davis fell back to the pack, cracking a mere 23 while slugging below .400. Alongside, both his exit velocity and hard-hit rate were much worse than normal. If there's good news, it's that Davis spent 2019 battling through a hand injury, which provides a reasonable explanation for the power outage. Still, there's reason to worry. As a DH with limited on-base skills, Davis only does one thing well. If the injury proves chronic or his pop doesn't return entirely, it's hard to justify his spot in the lineup—a troubling state of affairs for someone on the wrong side of 30. Hopefully 2019 was just a blip. The jaw-dropping bombs his merry-go-round swing produces are a true joy; baseball is simply better when Khrush Davis is on top of his game.

YEAR	TEAM	LVL	AGE	PA	DRC+	VORP	BABIP	BRR	FRAA	WARP
2017	OAK	MLB	29	652	123	34.1	.290	-0.2	LF(116): -8.9	2.5
2018	OAK	MLB	30	654	139	33.3	.261	-4.6	LF(11): -1.9	3.4
2019	OAK	MLB	31	533	91	2.5	.264	-1.6	LF(4): -0.3	0.1
2020	OAK	MLB	32	525	100	0.8	.274	-1.8	LF -2	-0.1

Khris Davis, continued

Batted Ball Distribution

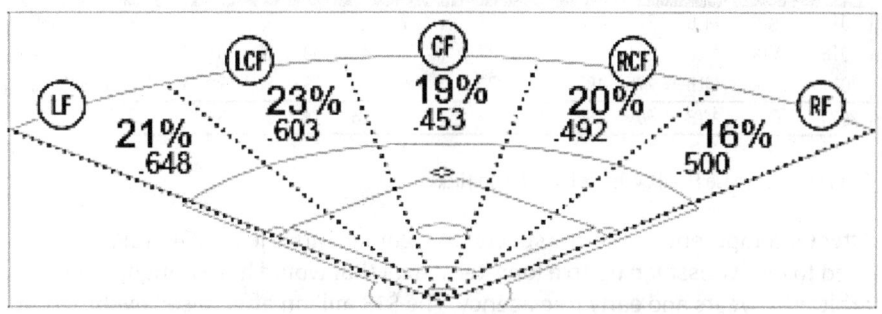

Strike Zone vs LHP   **Strike Zone vs RHP**

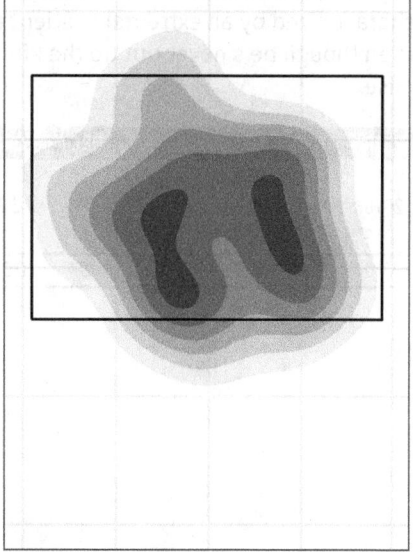

Robbie Grossman OF

Born: 09/16/89   Age: 30   Bats: B   Throws: L
Height: 6'0"   Weight: 215   Origin: Round 6, 2008 Draft (#174 overall)

YEAR	TEAM	LVL	AGE	PA	R	2B	3B	HR	RBI	BB	K	SB	CS	AVG/OBP/SLG
2017	MIN	MLB	27	456	62	22	1	9	45	67	79	3	1	.246/.361/.380
2018	MIN	MLB	28	465	50	27	1	5	48	60	83	0	1	.273/.367/.384
2019	OAK	MLB	29	482	57	21	3	6	38	59	86	9	4	.240/.334/.348
2020	OAK	MLB	30	280	28	12	1	5	26	36	56	3	1	.228/.331/.342

Comparables: Chase Headley, Travis Buck, Aaron Hicks

After 68 competent but hardly spectacular games with the 2013 Astros, Houston tried to lock Grossman up to a long-term deal that would have bought out his arbitration years and early free agency. The $13 million offer raised eyebrows at the time, and offered a hint at the direction baseball's marketplace was heading. In a depressing twist, Grossman has both been a better player than $13 million over six years should buy, and been paid less than that for his trouble. In any case, Grossman is a pretty easy guy to peg these days: He's a decent hitter characterized by an extremely patient approach that makes him a useful player, even though he's never put up the kind of counting numbers that leads to a big raise.

YEAR	TEAM	LVL	AGE	PA	DRC+	VORP	BABIP	BRR	FRAA	WARP
2017	MIN	MLB	27	456	99	5.5	.287	-1.9	RF(35): -1.6, LF(18): -1.2	0.3
2018	MIN	MLB	28	465	105	12.8	.329	-4.9	RF(52): -2.6, LF(34): 1.2	0.6
2019	OAK	MLB	29	482	97	11.2	.288	-4.3	LF(112): 3.2, RF(20): -1.3	0.9
2020	OAK	MLB	30	280	87	0.3	.278	-1.9	LF 3, RF -1	0.3

Robbie Grossman, continued

Batted Ball Distribution

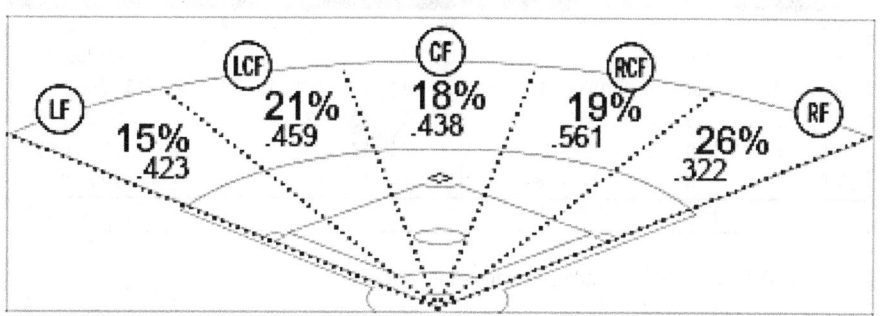

Strike Zone vs LHP **Strike Zone vs RHP**

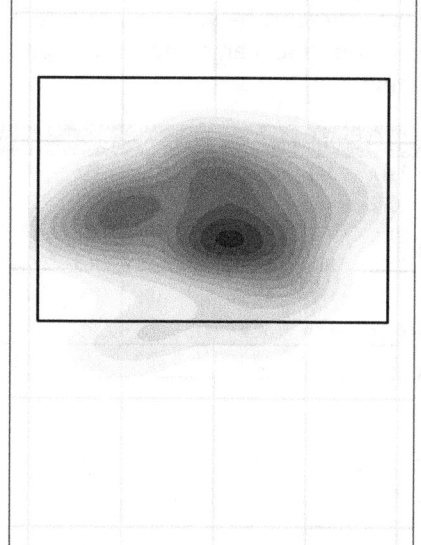

Tony Kemp UT

Born: 10/31/91 Age: 28 Bats: L Throws: R
Height: 5'6" Weight: 165 Origin: Round 5, 2013 Draft (#137 overall)

YEAR	TEAM	LVL	AGE	PA	R	2B	3B	HR	RBI	BB	K	SB	CS	AVG/OBP/SLG
2017	FRE	AAA	25	554	95	23	9	10	62	35	43	24	7	.329/.375/.470
2017	HOU	MLB	25	39	6	1	0	0	4	1	5	1	0	.216/.256/.243
2018	FRE	AAA	26	183	33	6	5	0	19	19	15	13	2	.335/.407/.435
2018	HOU	MLB	26	295	37	15	0	6	30	32	44	9	3	.263/.351/.392
2019	HOU	MLB	27	186	23	6	2	7	17	16	29	4	3	.227/.308/.417
2019	CHN	MLB	27	93	8	3	2	1	12	7	18	0	1	.183/.258/.305
2020	CHN	MLB	28	168	16	7	1	3	16	15	29	5	2	.232/.308/.363

Comparables: Johnny Giavotella, Adam Frazier, Jemile Weeks

Kemp is, at best, a handy end-of-bench utility type. We can all agree to that, and to him authoring one of the strangest sequences of the season in late September. If you missed it, he appeared to have struck out against Giovanny Gallegos…except Gallegos had been called for a balk, voiding the pitch result. On the next pitch—yes, the very next one—Kemp hit a go-ahead home run. We can't remember anything like it happening, which is to say, baseball is a cool game.

YEAR	TEAM	LVL	AGE	PA	DRC+	VORP	BABIP	BRR	FRAA	WARP
2017	FRE	AAA	25	554	112	40.4	.344	0.4	2B(97): -10.2, CF(10): -0.2	1.4
2017	HOU	MLB	25	39	91	-1.7	.250	0.9	LF(10): -0.4, CF(4): -0.2	0.1
2018	FRE	AAA	26	183	110	14.6	.367	3.5	2B(25): -0.5, CF(14): -1.4	1.0
2018	HOU	MLB	26	295	105	9.4	.296	-0.5	LF(61): -2.8, CF(32): 0.3	0.7
2019	HOU	MLB	27	186	100	5.7	.233	-1.1	2B(29): -0.9, LF(14): 0.7	0.4
2019	CHN	MLB	27	93	67	-1.2	.215	0.8	2B(14): 0.0, LF(6): 0.5	0.0
2020	CHN	MLB	28	168	79	1.6	.268	0.0	CF 0, 2B 0	0.1

Tony Kemp, continued

Batted Ball Distribution

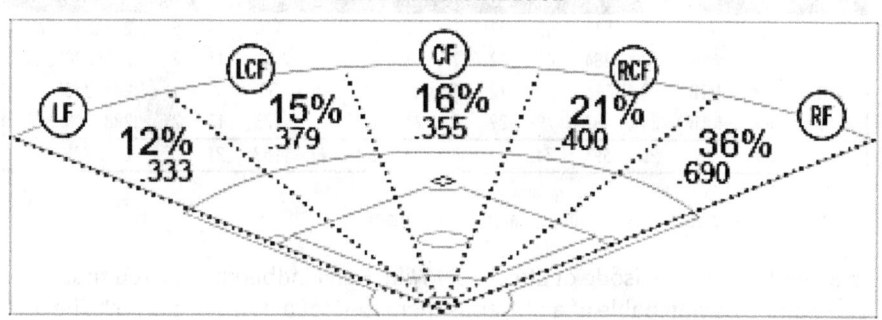

Strike Zone vs LHP   **Strike Zone vs RHP**

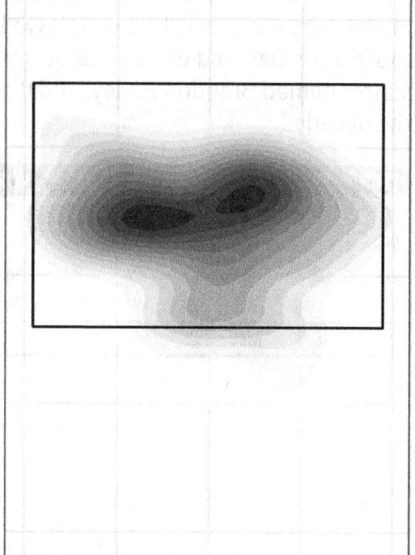

Oakland Athletics 2020

Ramón Laureano CF
Born: 07/15/94 Age: 25 Bats: R Throws: R
Height: 5'11" Weight: 200 Origin: Round 16, 2014 Draft (#466 overall)

YEAR	TEAM	LVL	AGE	PA	R	2B	3B	HR	RBI	BB	K	SB	CS	AVG/OBP/SLG
2017	CCH	AA	22	513	65	21	6	11	55	40	110	24	5	.227/.298/.369
2018	NAS	AAA	23	284	44	12	1	14	35	31	70	11	2	.297/.380/.524
2018	OAK	MLB	23	176	27	12	1	5	19	16	50	7	1	.288/.358/.474
2019	OAK	MLB	24	481	79	29	0	24	67	27	123	13	2	.288/.340/.521
2020	OAK	MLB	25	595	74	30	3	27	83	43	163	21	6	.259/.325/.471

Comparables: Chris Young, Brett Phillips, Aaron Cunningham

In an early-season episode of Effectively Wild, Ben Lindbergh declared that Laureano is as watchable of a player as there is—"for a non-star player." The first part held up, as he again dazzled with a sublime collection of moonshots, lasers, and tremendous catches, including a memorable home run robbery that preserved a no-hitter for Mike Fiers. But Laureano isn't just a ballplayer who shines occasionally anymore: He's a star in his own right. And in an era where big bashers run amok, Laureano's well-rounded game makes him a rare five-tool player. Oakland was somehow able to acquire this guy for a minor-league starter named Brandon Bailey, and it's turned into one of the low-key steals of the decade.

YEAR	TEAM	LVL	AGE	PA	DRC+	VORP	BABIP	BRR	FRAA	WARP
2017	CCH	AA	22	513	80	12.7	.273	6.3	RF(95): 7.8, CF(31): -1.7	1.6
2018	NAS	AAA	23	284	142	24.2	.358	1.7	RF(45): 6.2, CF(19): -0.5	2.9
2018	OAK	MLB	23	176	93	16.0	.388	1.4	CF(47): 3.0	0.9
2019	OAK	MLB	24	481	115	26.9	.342	2.2	CF(110): 9.0, RF(13): 5.1	4.2
2020	OAK	MLB	25	595	110	30.1	.323	1.6	CF 3, RF 1	3.4

Ramón Laureano, continued

Batted Ball Distribution

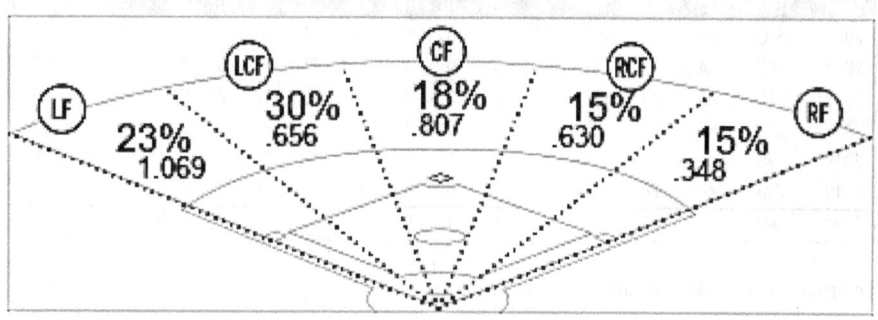

Strike Zone vs LHP   **Strike Zone vs RHP**

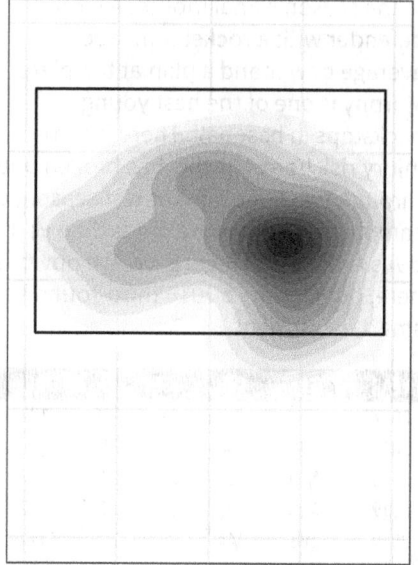

Oakland Athletics 2020

Sean Murphy   C

Born: 10/10/94   Age: 25   Bats: R   Throws: R
Height: 6'3"   Weight: 232   Origin: Round 3, 2016 Draft (#83 overall)

YEAR	TEAM	LVL	AGE	PA	R	2B	3B	HR	RBI	BB	K	SB	CS	AVG/OBP/SLG
2017	STO	A+	22	178	22	11	0	9	26	11	33	0	0	.297/.343/.527
2017	MID	AA	22	217	25	7	0	4	22	21	34	0	0	.209/.288/.309
2018	MID	AA	23	289	51	26	2	8	43	23	47	3	0	.288/.358/.498
2019	AGO	RK	24	32	8	2	0	1	1	4	4	0	0	.214/.313/.393
2019	LVG	AAA	24	140	25	6	1	10	30	15	31	0	1	.308/.386/.625
2019	OAK	MLB	24	60	14	5	0	4	8	6	16	0	0	.245/.333/.566
2020	OAK	MLB	25	385	43	18	1	16	50	31	98	1	0	.227/.297/.421

Comparables: J.T. Realmuto, Chris Parmelee, Ty France

Oakland's catcher of the future managed to stay just healthy enough to become the catcher of the present in the season's final month. A strong defender with a rocket arm, above-average power and a plan at the plate, Murphy is one of the best young backstops in baseball. There is some injury risk here: Murphy has broken both hamate bones and he had to battle through two knee injuries last season, one of which required surgery after the campaign. That's more dings than you'd like on anybody, much less one who dons the tools of ignorance. We obviously can't forecast a clean bill of health here, but Murphy's 2016 third-round selection is already looking like quite the smart investment.

YEAR	TEAM	P. COUNT	FRM RUNS	BLK RUNS	THRW RUNS	TOT RUNS
2017	MID	7267	3.6	-0.5	0.2	2.7
2018	MID	8864	13.6	1.4	0.6	15.6
2019	LVG	3998	1.1	0.2	-0.5	0.6
2019	OAK	2051	-0.2	-1.2	0.0	-1.4
2020	OAK	12807	-1.4	-2.8	0.1	-4.1

YEAR	TEAM	LVL	AGE	PA	DRC+	VORP	BABIP	BRR	FRAA	WARP
2017	STO	A+	22	178	132	15.1	.323	0.2	C(40): -0.3	1.3
2017	MID	AA	22	217	58	2.1	.232	0.6	C(51): 3.8	0.6
2018	MID	AA	23	289	137	22.5	.324	2.1	C(65): 14.5	4.2
2019	AGO	RK	24	32	122	0.0	.217	0.2	C(8): -0.1	0.2
2019	LVG	AAA	24	140	122	13.4	.329	-1.3	C(27): 1.5	1.0
2019	OAK	MLB	24	60	98	2.9	.273	1.1	C(18): -1.6	0.2
2020	OAK	MLB	25	385	90	11.1	.268	-0.6	C -4	0.7

Sean Murphy, continued

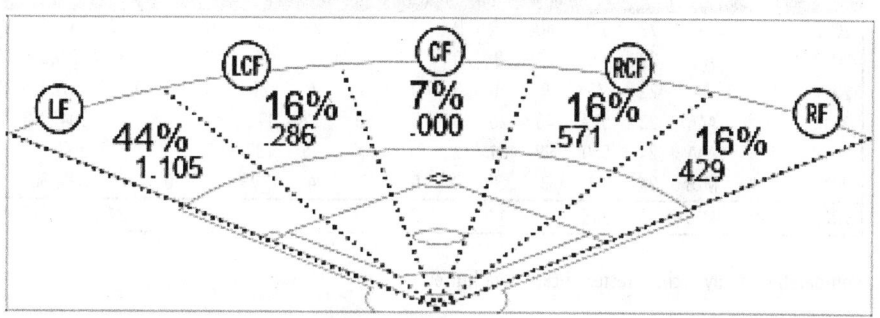

Batted Ball Distribution

Strike Zone vs LHP **Strike Zone vs RHP**

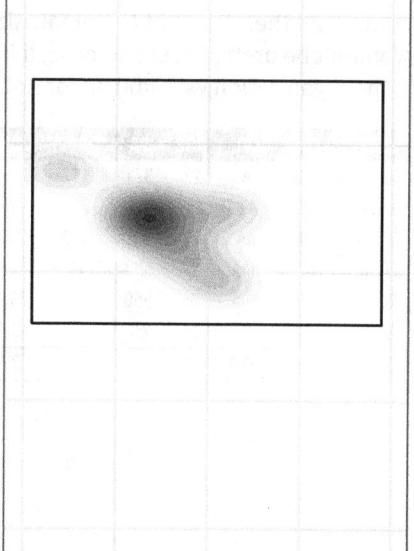

Oakland Athletics 2020

Sheldon Neuse 3B

Born: 12/10/94 Age: 25 Bats: R Throws: R
Height: 6'0" Weight: 218 Origin: Round 2, 2016 Draft (#58 overall)

YEAR	TEAM	LVL	AGE	PA	R	2B	3B	HR	RBI	BB	K	SB	CS	AVG/OBP/SLG
2017	HAG	A	22	321	40	19	3	9	51	25	66	12	5	.291/.349/.469
2017	STO	A+	22	94	21	3	0	7	22	9	25	2	0	.386/.457/.675
2017	MID	AA	22	75	9	4	0	0	6	6	21	0	0	.373/.427/.433
2018	NAS	AAA	23	537	48	26	3	5	55	32	172	4	1	.263/.304/.357
2019	LVG	AAA	24	560	99	31	2	27	102	56	132	3	3	.317/.389/.550
2019	OAK	MLB	24	61	3	3	0	0	7	4	19	0	0	.250/.295/.304
2020	OAK	MLB	25	245	24	11	1	7	27	17	73	1	1	.245/.302/.388

Comparables: Cody Asche, Preston Tucker, Trea Turner

The A's found out that when you bring Neuse to Oakland, you might also bring a funk. While the 25-year-old produced in the high-octane environs of the PCL (and particularly Las Vegas), he struggled upon arriving in the majors, failing to display the raw power he's known for. He's got the arm and body for the hot corner, but there's a Matt Chapman-sized roadblock there. The defense wouldn't be pretty at second base, if his bat can state his case for it. After all, this is the organization well-known for not selling jeans.

YEAR	TEAM	LVL	AGE	PA	DRC+	VORP	BABIP	BRR	FRAA	WARP
2017	HAG	A	22	321	147	26.7	.347	-1.9	SS(43): -2.9, 3B(33): 6.6	3.0
2017	STO	A+	22	94	217	17.0	.490	0.4	3B(10): -1.5, SS(8): -0.4	1.3
2017	MID	AA	22	75	142	4.9	.532	0.3	3B(18): 1.4, 1B(1): -0.4	0.7
2018	NAS	AAA	23	537	77	11.4	.385	-0.4	3B(130): -3.1, 2B(1): 0.0	0.2
2019	LVG	AAA	24	560	117	39.2	.384	0.3	3B(96): 12.3, 2B(15): 0.6	4.4
2019	OAK	MLB	24	61	70	-0.4	.368	0.3	2B(20): -1.4, 3B(5): -0.3	-0.2
2020	OAK	MLB	25	245	82	3.2	.333	-0.3	2B -2, SS 0	0.2

Sheldon Neuse, continued

Batted Ball Distribution

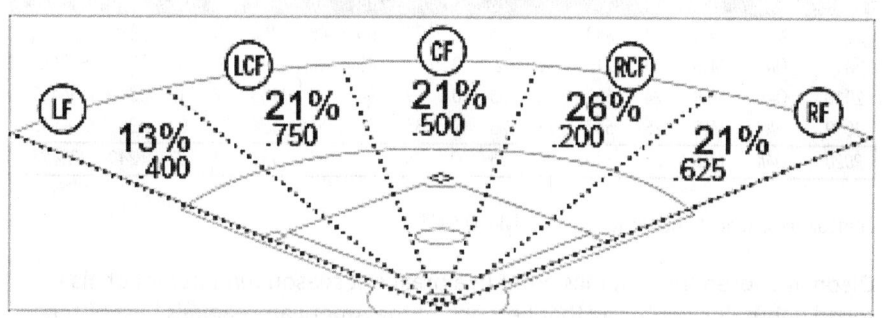

Strike Zone vs LHP   **Strike Zone vs RHP**

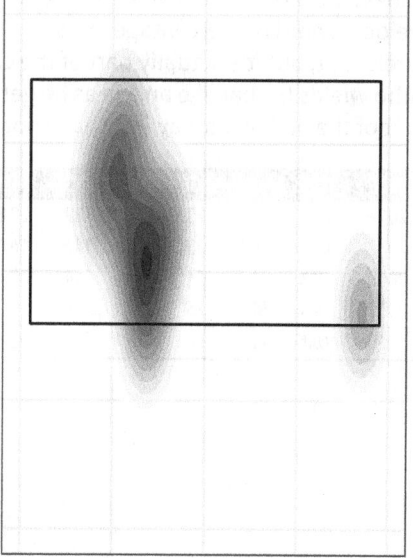

Athletics Player Analysis - 35

Oakland Athletics 2020

Matt Olson 1B

Born: 03/29/94 Age: 26 Bats: L Throws: R
Height: 6'5" Weight: 230 Origin: Round 1, 2012 Draft (#47 overall)

YEAR	TEAM	LVL	AGE	PA	R	2B	3B	HR	RBI	BB	K	SB	CS	AVG/OBP/SLG
2017	NAS	AAA	23	343	56	16	1	23	60	45	83	3	0	.272/.367/.568
2017	OAK	MLB	23	216	33	2	0	24	45	22	60	0	0	.259/.352/.651
2018	OAK	MLB	24	660	85	33	0	29	84	70	163	2	1	.247/.335/.453
2019	OAK	MLB	25	547	73	26	0	36	91	51	138	0	0	.267/.351/.545
2020	OAK	MLB	26	595	81	25	0	35	94	64	155	1	0	.240/.332/.491

Comparables: Randal Grichuk, Kyle Blanks, Tyler O'Neill

Olson anchored the Athletics order in a breakout season reminiscent of his torrid debut. It's fair to say that he's one of the American League's best hitters now (11th in DRC+ among qualifying hitters), and he would have made his first All-Star team if he hadn't missed 30-odd games after breaking his hamate bone in Japan. For an injury that often saps a player's power for months, Olson looked no worse for wear, finishing near the top of the charts in wOBA, exit velocity, hard hit percentage, muscle density... That last one may sound irrelevant, but it's actually part of the charm here: He's just a massive person who wields his bat like an axe as he gets ready to hit, and then whacks the crap out of the ball on its way in. What's not to love?

YEAR	TEAM	LVL	AGE	PA	DRC+	VORP	BABIP	BRR	FRAA	WARP
2017	NAS	AAA	23	343	139	29.8	.298	-0.1	1B(73): -0.8, 3B(1): -0.2	2.0
2017	OAK	MLB	23	216	146	16.1	.238	0.3	1B(43): 4.7, RF(12): 2.7	2.4
2018	OAK	MLB	24	660	114	20.6	.292	-2.6	1B(162): 3.8	2.2
2019	OAK	MLB	25	547	134	32.7	.300	-1.9	1B(127): 11.7	4.1
2020	OAK	MLB	26	595	121	26.5	.272	-1.4	1B 5	3.3

Matt Olson, continued

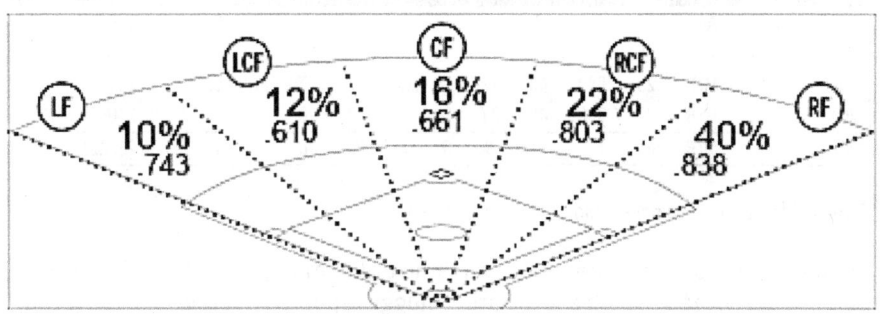

Strike Zone vs LHP   **Strike Zone vs RHP**

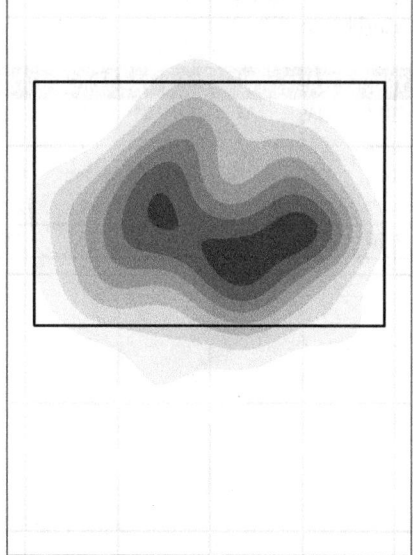

Oakland Athletics 2020

Chad Pinder   UT

Born: 03/29/92   Age: 28   Bats: R   Throws: R
Height: 6'2"   Weight: 207   Origin: Round 2, 2013 Draft (#71 overall)

YEAR	TEAM	LVL	AGE	PA	R	2B	3B	HR	RBI	BB	K	SB	CS	AVG/OBP/SLG
2017	NAS	AAA	25	71	3	2	1	1	2	6	23	2	1	.266/.338/.375
2017	OAK	MLB	25	309	36	15	1	15	42	18	92	2	1	.238/.292/.457
2018	OAK	MLB	26	333	43	12	1	13	27	27	88	0	2	.258/.332/.436
2019	OAK	MLB	27	370	45	21	0	13	47	20	88	0	1	.240/.290/.416
2020	OAK	MLB	28	175	19	8	0	7	22	10	44	1	0	.232/.289/.410

Comparables: Danny Espinosa, Jedd Gyorko, Jason Kipnis

Pinder is perhaps the game's most versatile utility man these days, a bit of an odd role for someone with a .432 career slugging percentage. He again saw time at every position besides catcher and pitcher, starting at least once everywhere except short. His career trajectory appears set now, as he's basically baseball's Jonathan Isaac: not quite reliable enough on offense for a starring role, but too valuable and versatile defensively to get traded. There are worse fates a man could have.

YEAR	TEAM	LVL	AGE	PA	DRC+	VORP	BABIP	BRR	FRAA	WARP
2017	NAS	AAA	25	71	77	0.7	.400	-1.5	2B(8): 0.1, SS(4): -0.3	-0.2
2017	OAK	MLB	25	309	97	7.6	.292	-1.8	RF(35): -0.5, SS(22): 1.6	0.8
2018	OAK	MLB	26	333	110	15.4	.325	0.8	LF(64): 4.8, 2B(21): -1.3	1.8
2019	OAK	MLB	27	370	82	2.0	.284	0.9	LF(46): 2.4, RF(34): 4.2	0.7
2020	OAK	MLB	28	175	84	1.9	.278	0.1	2B -1, LF 2	0.3

Chad Pinder, continued

Batted Ball Distribution

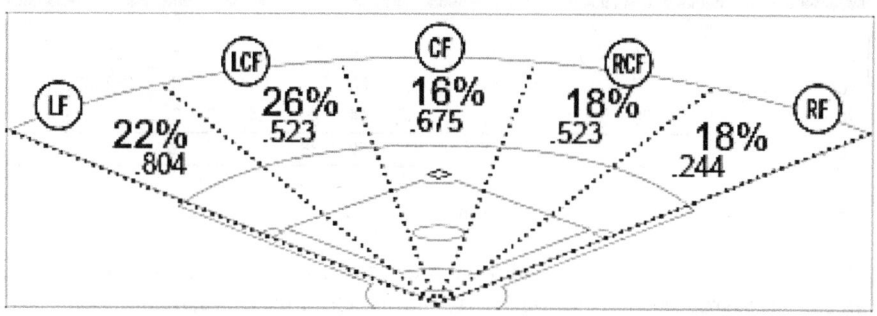

Strike Zone vs LHP   **Strike Zone vs RHP**

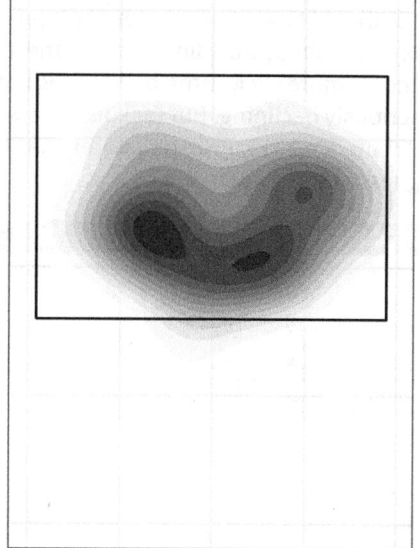

Oakland Athletics 2020

Stephen Piscotty   RF

Born: 01/14/91   Age: 29   Bats: R   Throws: R
Height: 6'4"   Weight: 205   Origin: Round 1, 2012 Draft (#36 overall)

YEAR	TEAM	LVL	AGE	PA	R	2B	3B	HR	RBI	BB	K	SB	CS	AVG/OBP/SLG
2017	MEM	AAA	26	38	7	3	0	4	7	6	7	0	0	.313/.421/.781
2017	SLN	MLB	26	401	40	16	1	9	39	52	87	3	6	.235/.342/.367
2018	OAK	MLB	27	605	78	41	0	27	88	42	114	2	0	.267/.331/.491
2019	OAK	MLB	28	393	46	17	1	13	44	29	84	2	0	.249/.309/.412
2020	OAK	MLB	29	455	53	24	1	17	59	38	101	4	2	.253/.324/.444

Comparables: Greg Luzinski, Ryan Klesko, Mike Shannon

After his second subpar season at the plate in three tries, Piscotty's career is at an early crossroads. There've been extenuating circumstances, including a melanoma scare and a bad ankle sprain last year, but at the end of the day he has only notched 2.7 WARP over the last three years combined. Twenty-nine now, he's not much of a defender, and he's at risk of falling down Oakland's pecking order in the outfield. The tradeoff of more swing-and-miss for additional power is one a lot of players have made, but Piscotty's extra whiffs brought about a decline in ISO. If there's a positive here, it's that Piscotty has shown more stick in the past, and is not yet at an age where you'd think he's seriously declining. But for someone who hit the ground running when he debuted in 2015, Piscotty's career has been more turbulent than we'd have guessed three years ago.

YEAR	TEAM	LVL	AGE	PA	DRC+	VORP	BABIP	BRR	FRAA	WARP
2017	MEM	AAA	26	38	180	7.0	.286	0.0	RF(6): -0.2	0.4
2017	SLN	MLB	26	401	95	1.9	.286	-2.5	RF(99): -0.9	0.3
2018	OAK	MLB	27	605	120	28.0	.290	-1.4	RF(151): -9.3	1.7
2019	OAK	MLB	28	393	95	6.5	.289	1.1	RF(90): -3.7	0.4
2020	OAK	MLB	29	455	103	10.8	.296	-0.6	RF -2	0.9

Stephen Piscotty, continued

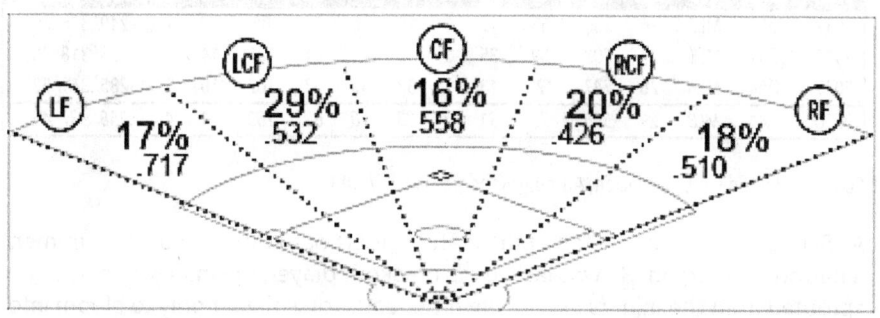

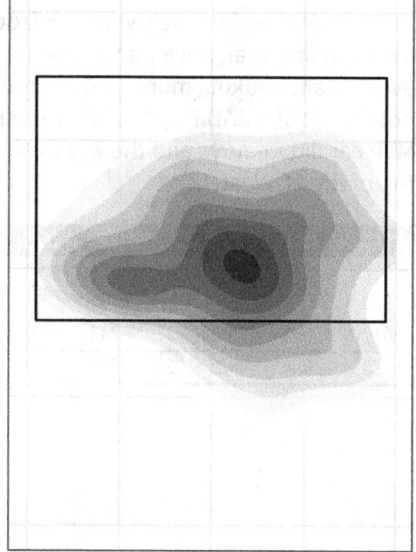

Oakland Athletics 2020

Marcus Semien SS
Born: 09/17/90   Age: 29   Bats: R   Throws: R
Height: 6'0"   Weight: 195   Origin: Round 6, 2011 Draft (#201 overall)

YEAR	TEAM	LVL	AGE	PA	R	2B	3B	HR	RBI	BB	K	SB	CS	AVG/OBP/SLG
2017	OAK	MLB	26	386	53	19	1	10	40	38	85	12	1	.249/.325/.398
2018	OAK	MLB	27	703	89	35	2	15	70	61	131	14	6	.255/.318/.388
2019	OAK	MLB	28	747	123	43	7	33	92	87	102	10	8	.285/.369/.522
2020	OAK	MLB	29	595	72	31	3	23	78	62	103	11	4	.258/.337/.455

Comparables: Edwin Encarnación, Anthony Rendon, David Wright

As Semien hung near the top of the WARP leaderboard throughout the summer, a narrative emerged: He was last year's breakout player, the man who had sprouted from the minors as a feeble hitter and worse fielder only to bloom into a star late in his prime. The sentiment is mostly right, particularly defensively where he's transformed into one of the league's finest fielders at an age most shortstops begin warily eyeing third base. But while 2019 might be his statistical summit, Semien's ascendency to stardom has been far more linear than most assume. At the plate, he's shown a Troutian ability to enhance his game with each passing year. Power and patience came first, and now he's hitting for average and making more contact, too. Whether he's done growing or not—short of a BABIP spike, he's running out of things to get batter at—he's an MVP candidate now, and the key to any potential for a passing of the torch at the top of the AL West.

YEAR	TEAM	LVL	AGE	PA	DRC+	VORP	BABIP	BRR	FRAA	WARP
2017	OAK	MLB	26	386	94	19.0	.300	3.9	SS(85): -1.5	1.7
2018	OAK	MLB	27	703	99	37.5	.296	5.4	SS(159): 16.2	5.4
2019	OAK	MLB	28	747	135	70.6	.294	1.8	SS(161): 4.2	7.5
2020	OAK	MLB	29	595	109	32.6	.281	3.0	SS 6	4.0

Marcus Semien, continued

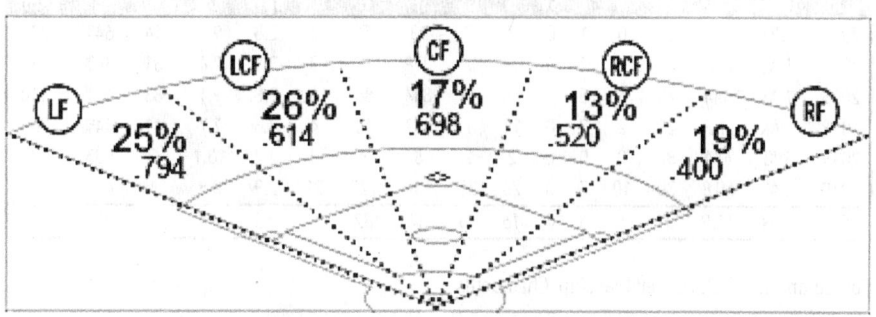

Batted Ball Distribution

Strike Zone vs LHP   **Strike Zone vs RHP**

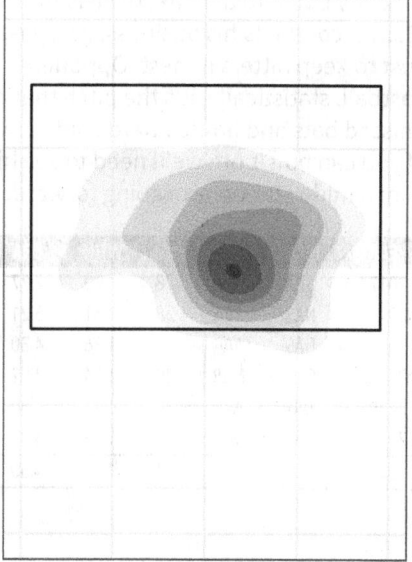

Chris Bassitt RHP

Born: 02/22/89 Age: 31 Bats: R Throws: R
Height: 6'5" Weight: 220 Origin: Round 16, 2011 Draft (#501 overall)

YEAR	TEAM	LVL	AGE	W	L	SV	G	GS	IP	H	HR	BB/9	K/9	K	GB%	BABIP
2017	STO	A+	28	0	1	0	7	7	13	9	0	2.8	9.7	14	64%	.273
2017	NAS	AAA	28	4	2	0	17	2	37^2	41	3	3.8	7.4	31	36%	.336
2018	NAS	AAA	29	5	5	0	18	14	81^2	86	6	2.8	9.1	83	44%	.348
2018	OAK	MLB	29	2	3	0	11	7	47^2	40	4	3.6	7.7	41	44%	.265
2019	LVG	AAA	30	0	0	0	2	2	8	8	2	2.2	10.1	9	58%	.273
2019	OAK	MLB	30	10	5	0	28	25	144	125	21	2.9	8.8	141	42%	.267
2020	OAK	MLB	31	6	5	0	16	16	84	82	12	3.3	8.4	79	43%	.296

Comparables: Erik Davis, Jeff Manship, Chad Bettis

In a relic from the Moneyball days, the A's remain proficient at squeezing magic from obscure 30-year-olds. Bassitt is the latest rabbit out of the hat. He only appeared 18 times from 2016-2018 but started 25 games last year, riding a velocity boost to a breakout season. There's not much mystery about how Bassitt conducts his business: gas, gas, more gas and the occasional slow curve just to keep hitters honest. Opponents had a typically difficult time with the fastball: statistically, it's the pitch that most batters hit hardest but Bassitt both missed bats and limited hard contact with the ol' number one. That's a nice trick if you can pull it off; we'll need to see him do it again before comfortably calling him a mid-rotation arm going forward.

YEAR	TEAM	LVL	AGE	WHIP	ERA	DRA	WARP	MPH	FB%	WHF	CSP
2017	STO	A+	28	1.00	2.77	3.02	0.3				
2017	NAS	AAA	28	1.51	6.21	5.05	0.1				
2018	NAS	AAA	29	1.36	4.30	4.15	1.2				
2018	OAK	MLB	29	1.24	3.02	5.24	0.0	94.7	57.4	7.6	51.8
2019	LVG	AAA	30	1.25	4.50	2.60	0.3				
2019	OAK	MLB	30	1.19	3.81	4.45	2.0	95.8	64.9	9.7	51.9
2020	OAK	MLB	31	1.35	4.50	4.69	0.8	94.7	62.9	9.2	51.6

Chris Bassitt, continued

Pitch Shape vs LHH

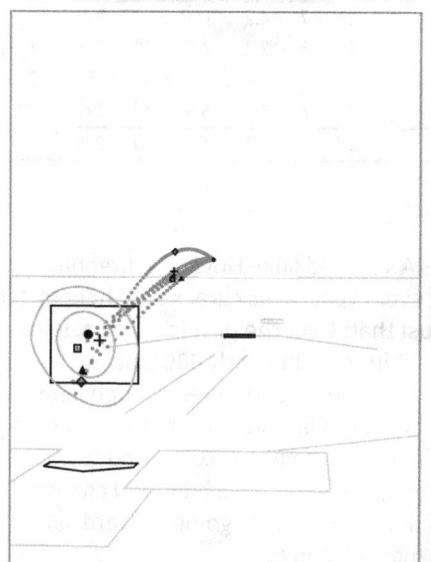

Pitch Shape vs RHH

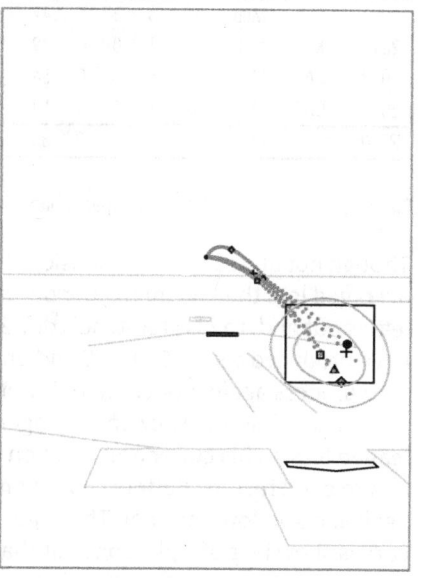

Type	Frequency	Velocity	H Movement	V Movement
● Fastball	24.2%	94.3 [105]	-7.5 [97]	-15 [102]
□ Sinker	40.7%	93.5 [104]	-13.4 [95]	-18.6 [106]
+ Cutter	13.8%	88.7 [100]	2.1 [101]	-24.4 [99]
▲ Changeup	8.4%	85.3 [100]	-14.6 [84]	-25.2 [106]
✕ Splitter				
▽ Slider				
◇ Curveball	12.8%	70.6 [74]	12.9 [122]	-62.5 [68]
⊕ Slow Curveball				
✳ Knuckleball				
▼ Screwball				

Oakland Athletics 2020

Ryan Buchter   LHP
Born: 02/13/87   Age: 33   Bats: L   Throws: L
Height: 6'4"   Weight: 232   Origin: Round 33, 2005 Draft (#984 overall)

YEAR	TEAM	LVL	AGE	W	L	SV	G	GS	IP	H	HR	BB/9	K/9	K	GB%	BABIP
2017	SDN	MLB	30	3	3	1	42	0	38¹	28	7	4.2	11.0	47	33%	.239
2017	KCA	MLB	30	1	0	0	29	0	27	16	3	2.7	6.0	18	32%	.173
2018	OAK	MLB	31	6	0	0	54	0	39¹	32	4	3.4	9.4	41	28%	.272
2019	OAK	MLB	32	1	1	0	64	0	45¹	42	8	4.6	9.9	50	29%	.296
2020	OAK	MLB	33	2	2	0	33	0	35	29	6	4.1	8.9	35	29%	.262

Comparables: Sam Freeman, Clay Rapada, Dan Runzler

Though not quite as one-dimensional as A's legend Mike Holtz, Buchter has averaged less than an inning per outing every year of his career. He's here to get lefties out and, to his credit, he's done just that: Over the past four years, lefties have produced a sub-.600 OPS and only 10 homers in nearly 400 plate appearances against Buchter. He's not so good against righties, though, and that's troubling since he can no longer come in to face just one batter. Buchter leaned less on his cutter and more on his curve last year as compared to 2018, and to good results: Batters couldn't manage an extra-base hit in 170 chances against his yellow hammer. That's good news for Buchter going forward, as curves show less of a platoon split than most offerings.

YEAR	TEAM	LVL	AGE	WHIP	ERA	DRA	WARP	MPH	FB%	WHF	CSP
2017	SDN	MLB	30	1.20	3.05	5.03	0.1	94.8	72.1	12.7	47.3
2017	KCA	MLB	30	0.89	2.67	5.67	-0.2	94.4	72.1	10.3	49.8
2018	OAK	MLB	31	1.19	2.75	3.60	0.6	94.6	65.7	12.2	48.1
2019	OAK	MLB	32	1.43	2.98	5.94	-0.3	94.7	64.1	12.3	46.4
2020	OAK	MLB	33	1.29	4.00	4.24	0.4	93.6	66.4	11.9	46.9

Ryan Buchter, continued

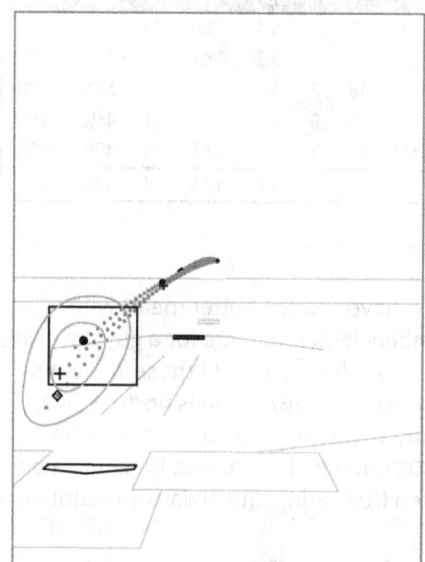

Pitch Shape vs LHH

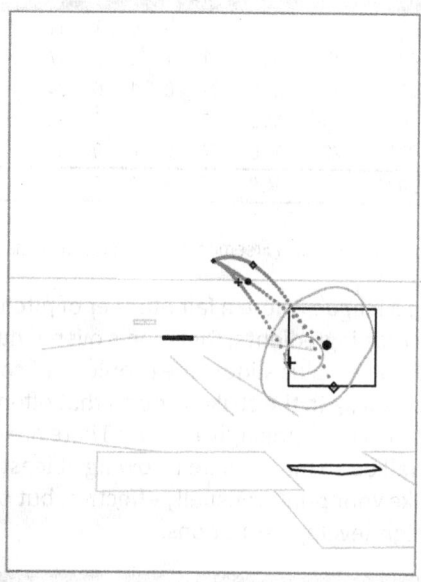

Pitch Shape vs RHH

Type	Frequency	Velocity	H Movement	V Movement
● Fastball	62.8%	92.9 [101]	7.8 [96]	-12.5 [109]
☐ Sinker				
+ Cutter	13.4%	89.9 [107]	0.7 [85]	-19.3 [118]
▲ Changeup				
✕ Splitter				
▽ Slider				
◇ Curveball	20.9%	78 [98]	-13.4 [124]	-43.9 [108]
⊕ Slow Curveball				
✱ Knuckleball				
▼ Screwball				

Jake Diekman LHP

Born: 01/21/87 Age: 33 Bats: L Throws: L
Height: 6'4" Weight: 200 Origin: Round 30, 2007 Draft (#923 overall)

YEAR	TEAM	LVL	AGE	W	L	SV	G	GS	IP	H	HR	BB/9	K/9	K	GB%	BABIP
2017	TEX	MLB	30	0	0	1	11	0	10²	4	1	8.4	11.0	13	59%	.143
2018	TEX	MLB	31	1	1	2	47	0	39	31	2	5.3	11.1	48	48%	.302
2018	ARI	MLB	31	0	1	0	24	0	14¹	18	2	5.0	11.3	18	57%	.400
2019	OAK	MLB	32	1	1	0	28	0	20¹	16	0	7.1	9.3	21	46%	.296
2019	KCA	MLB	32	0	6	0	48	0	41²	33	3	5.0	13.6	63	49%	.330
2020	OAK	MLB	33	3	2	0	49	0	52	41	5	4.7	11.5	66	48%	.295

Comparables: Sam Freeman, Mike Dunn, Kevin Chapman

In a league where a fair number of pitchers have cooked better meals with worse ingredients, Diekman's overall numbers look mediocre for a guy throwing 98 with a plus slider. The problem, of course, is that neither of those weapons winds up in the strike zone all that often. His career BB/9 ratio is north of five, which is surprisingly rare air: There are only 13 pitchers this century who have walked so many while throwing at least 300 innings. That makes Diekman a bit like your printer: usually effective, but often frustrating and always stressful in high-leverage situations.

YEAR	TEAM	LVL	AGE	WHIP	ERA	DRA	WARP	MPH	FB%	WHF	CSP
2017	TEX	MLB	30	1.31	2.53	7.02	-0.2	97.8	68.1	12.2	37.4
2018	TEX	MLB	31	1.38	3.69	6.34	-0.6	97.2	62.4	11.4	45.4
2018	ARI	MLB	31	1.81	7.53	6.25	-0.2	97.6	67.9	13.5	46.8
2019	OAK	MLB	32	1.57	4.43	4.81	0.1	97.5	59.1	12.2	46.8
2019	KCA	MLB	32	1.34	4.75	2.69	1.2	97.9	51	17.7	47.5
2020	OAK	MLB	33	1.32	3.78	3.91	0.7	96.5	57.7	14	43.8

Jake Diekman, continued

Pitch Shape vs LHH

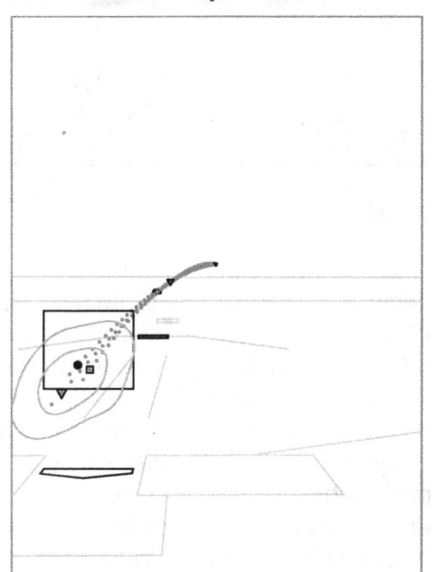

Pitch Shape vs RHH

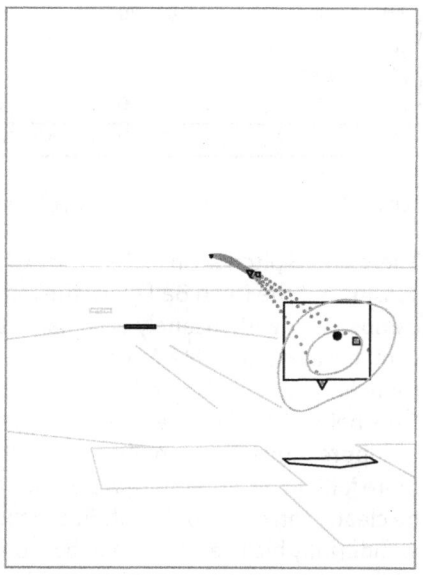

Type	Frequency	Velocity	H Movement	V Movement
● Fastball	47.7%	96.2 [111]	12.5 [75]	-16.7 [98]
☐ Sinker	6.0%	95.9 [117]	15.3 [83]	-20.9 [98]
+ Cutter				
▲ Changeup				
✕ Splitter				
▽ Slider	46.0%	85.4 [104]	-4.8 [99]	-35.9 [92]
◇ Curveball				
⊕ Slow Curveball				
✱ Knuckleball				
▼ Screwball				

Athletics Player Analysis - 49

Oakland Athletics 2020

Mike Fiers RHP

Born: 06/15/85 Age: 35 Bats: R Throws: R
Height: 6'2" Weight: 202 Origin: Round 22, 2009 Draft (#676 overall)

YEAR	TEAM	LVL	AGE	W	L	SV	G	GS	IP	H	HR	BB/9	K/9	K	GB%	BABIP
2017	HOU	MLB	32	8	10	0	29	28	153[1]	157	32	3.6	8.6	146	43%	.300
2018	DET	MLB	33	7	6	0	21	21	119	121	20	2.0	6.6	87	39%	.277
2018	OAK	MLB	33	5	2	0	10	9	53	45	12	1.9	8.8	52	43%	.246
2019	OAK	MLB	34	15	4	0	33	33	184[2]	166	30	2.6	6.1	126	40%	.254
2020	OAK	MLB	35	10	9	0	29	29	152	157	31	2.8	6.8	114	40%	.280

Comparables: Marco Estrada, Jeff Samardzija, Collin McHugh

There are 35 pitchers in MLB history who have thrown multiple no-hitters. Tossing out the Dead Ball guys, the remaining 25 or so break down into two camps: Guys with insanely dominant stuff and everyone else. The former group contains luminaries like Sandy Koufax, Nolan Ryan, and Randy Johnson, with room for folks who burned brightly but quickly: Jim Maloney, Jake Arrieta, etc. Fiers belongs to the latter cohort, a soft-tosser for his day, and not one too adept at suppressing hits normally. That isn't to say he isn't good: Whether you place more faith in his ho-hum DRA's or moderately better ERA figures in recent years, he clearly can get people out. But the no-hitters are as shocking as they seem, a wonderfully bizarre example of baseball's ceaseless capacity to surprise. And while we're on surprises: Who would have guessed that Fiers, a member of the Astros' 2017 World Series team, would go on record about his discomfort with Houston's sign stealing system? His public account did much to spur MLB's investigation into Houston; we don't know the full ramifications of that investigation or how it will affect Fiers and his legacy, but the guess at press time is that the fallout will be substantial.

YEAR	TEAM	LVL	AGE	WHIP	ERA	DRA	WARP	MPH	FB%	WHF	CSP
2017	HOU	MLB	32	1.43	5.22	5.82	-0.4	91.9	47.5	9.9	46.6
2018	DET	MLB	33	1.24	3.48	4.87	0.6	91.6	51.4	8.8	49.1
2018	OAK	MLB	33	1.06	3.74	4.02	0.8	92.5	51.4	10.1	50.9
2019	OAK	MLB	34	1.19	3.90	5.06	1.4	92.6	51.8	8.6	49.8
2020	OAK	MLB	35	1.35	4.89	5.12	0.8	91.0	49.7	8.9	48

Mike Fiers, continued

Pitch Shape vs LHH

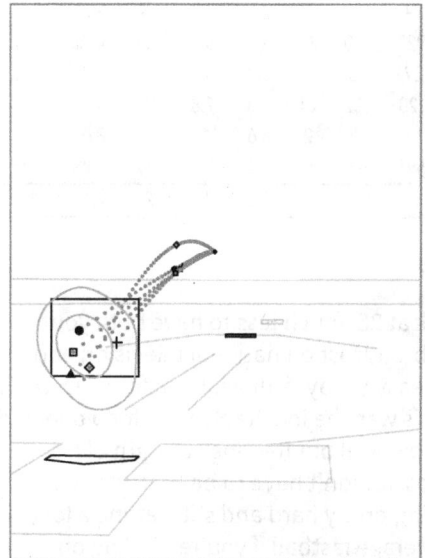

Pitch Shape vs RHH

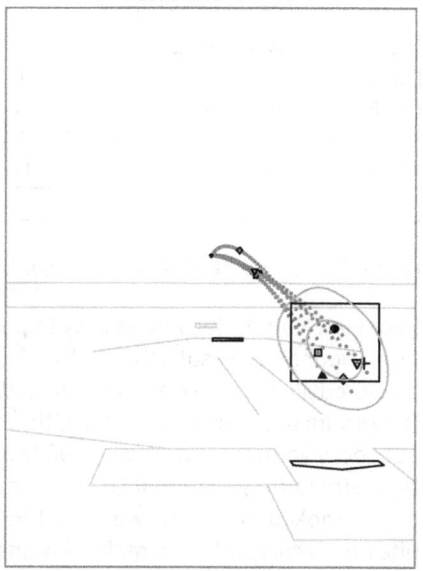

Type	Frequency	Velocity	H Movement	V Movement
● Fastball	31.1%	90.8 [96]	-7.2 [99]	-13.5 [106]
□ Sinker	20.7%	90.4 [89]	-12.8 [99]	-18.3 [107]
+ Cutter	15.3%	86.5 [86]	2.6 [104]	-23.4 [102]
▲ Changeup	12.4%	84.4 [97]	-13.2 [91]	-28.7 [96]
✕ Splitter				
▽ Slider	3.1%	84.5 [100]	5.6 [103]	-29.4 [111]
◇ Curveball	17.4%	74.4 [86]	10.4 [112]	-61.6 [70]
✪ Slow Curveball				
✱ Knuckleball				
▼ Screwball				

Oakland Athletics 2020

Matt Harvey RHP

Born: 03/27/89 Age: 31 Bats: R Throws: R
Height: 6'4" Weight: 220 Origin: Round 1, 2010 Draft (#7 overall)

YEAR	TEAM	LVL	AGE	W	L	SV	G	GS	IP	H	HR	BB/9	K/9	K	GB%	BABIP
2017	BIN	AA	28	0	0	0	2	2	7^2	9	1	2.3	5.9	5	33%	.308
2017	NYN	MLB	28	5	7	0	19	18	92^2	110	21	4.6	6.5	67	46%	.307
2018	NYN	MLB	29	0	2	0	8	4	27	33	6	3.0	6.7	20	43%	.310
2018	CIN	MLB	29	7	7	0	24	24	128	132	21	2.0	7.8	111	46%	.296
2019	LVG	AAA	30	1	0	0	5	3	17	13	2	2.6	11.1	21	37%	.282
2019	LAA	MLB	30	3	5	0	12	12	59^2	63	13	4.4	5.9	39	44%	.275
2020	OAK	MLB	31	2	2	0	33	0	35	38	7	3.3	7.0	27	43%	.297

Comparables: Chris Archer, Kyle Hendricks, Tyson Ross

Poor Matt Harvey. It can't be easy to peak at 26, much less to have both your finest hour and the subsequent free-fall broadcast on national television and plastered all over the New York Post. It's easy to say, four years on from Harvey's last productive season in Queens, that this was the inevitable path for a talented but cocky young star who relied on the powerful but fleeting strength of his right arm to roast National League lineups. It didn't have to be that way: When he first looked mortal, he was still throwing pretty hard and still getting a lot of bite on his curve. Harvey maintains an average fastball if you're grading on velocity alone, but it's trending in the wrong direction. His heater fell another tick in 2019, when he was more or less the worst pitcher in the league over 12 starts until the Angels finally threw in the towel. The A's picked him up as Homer Bailey insurance, in a sentence that would have made as much sense while invoking a lot less sadness back in 2013. The stuff is mediocre now, the execution is far worse and the trajectory is not promising. A dark night, indeed.

YEAR	TEAM	LVL	AGE	WHIP	ERA	DRA	WARP	MPH	FB%	WHF	CSP
2017	BIN	AA	28	1.43	5.87	4.85	0.0				
2017	NYN	MLB	28	1.69	6.70	6.63	-1.1	96.4	59.3	8.6	47
2018	NYN	MLB	29	1.56	7.00	4.18	0.3	95.3	61.2	8.2	49.7
2018	CIN	MLB	29	1.25	4.50	4.79	0.7	96.7	58.7	10.4	53
2019	LVG	AAA	30	1.06	3.18	5.35	0.2				
2019	LAA	MLB	30	1.54	7.09	7.62	-1.2	95.7	47.6	9.9	48.2
2020	OAK	MLB	31	1.45	5.37	5.38	-0.1	95.4	56.1	9.6	49

Matt Harvey, continued

Pitch Shape vs LHH	Pitch Shape vs RHH
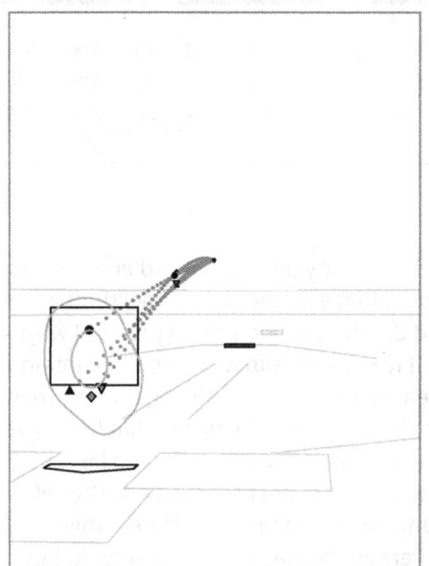	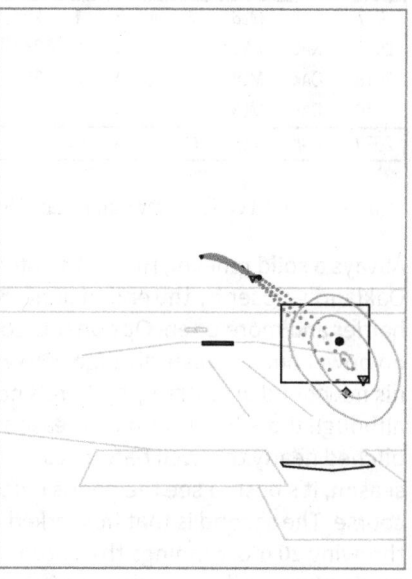

Type	Frequency	Velocity	H Movement	V Movement
● Fastball	44.3%	93.6 [103]	-10.1 [86]	-15.5 [101]
☐ Sinker	3.3%	94.4 [110]	-9.9 [118]	-17.6 [110]
+ Cutter				
▲ Changeup	10.3%	86.4 [104]	-12.1 [96]	-22.8 [113]
✕ Splitter				
▽ Slider	27.7%	87.8 [114]	2.5 [89]	-27.1 [117]
◇ Curveball	14.4%	82 [111]	3 [82]	-42.4 [111]
⊕ Slow Curveball				
✻ Knuckleball				
▼ Screwball				

Oakland Athletics 2020

Liam Hendriks   RHP

Born: 02/10/89   Age: 31   Bats: R   Throws: R
Height: 6'0"   Weight: 225   Origin: International Free Agent, 2007

YEAR	TEAM	LVL	AGE	W	L	SV	G	GS	IP	H	HR	BB/9	K/9	K	GB%	BABIP
2017	OAK	MLB	28	4	2	1	70	0	64	57	7	3.2	11.0	78	41%	.303
2018	NAS	AAA	29	4	1	6	23	1	25¹	21	1	1.4	15.3	43	41%	.364
2018	OAK	MLB	29	0	1	0	25	8	24	25	3	3.8	8.2	22	41%	.324
2019	OAK	MLB	30	4	4	25	75	2	85	61	5	2.2	13.1	124	32%	.311
2020	OAK	MLB	31	3	3	38	60	0	63	52	7	2.3	11.9	84	35%	.303

Comparables: Brett Cecil, Tommy Hunter, Zach McAllister

Always a solid reliever, Hendriks notched a career year in 2019 and emerged as Oakland's closer by the end of June. Key for him was the slider, now thrown harder and more often. Opponents could barely touch it, hitting just .114 with no power and an absurdly high 29% whiff rate on the pitch. If he can maintain his newfound arm strength, there's no reason he can't be filthy again next year, although there are a couple of reasons to be cautious. The first is that he's never pitched nearly this well before; as with Blake Treinen and Lou Trivino last season, it's best to see the goods twice before we expect them as a matter of course. The second is that he worked quite hard, appearing 75 times while throwing 20 more innings than normal. Perhaps he has the stamina for it, but that's a lot of miles for a guy in his 30s. That isn't to say Hendriks won't be good again this season, of course: Just don't be shocked if 2019 was the peak.

YEAR	TEAM	LVL	AGE	WHIP	ERA	DRA	WARP	MPH	FB%	WHF	CSP
2017	OAK	MLB	28	1.25	4.22	3.45	1.2	96.7	74.1	13.6	46.7
2018	NAS	AAA	29	0.99	2.84	2.03	0.9				
2018	OAK	MLB	29	1.46	4.12	4.70	0.1	97.7	70.1	12.1	47.1
2019	OAK	MLB	30	0.96	1.80	2.73	2.4	98.8	70.6	18.7	48.6
2020	OAK	MLB	31	1.07	2.70	3.13	1.4	97.2	71.1	16.1	47.3

Liam Hendriks, continued

Pitch Shape vs LHH

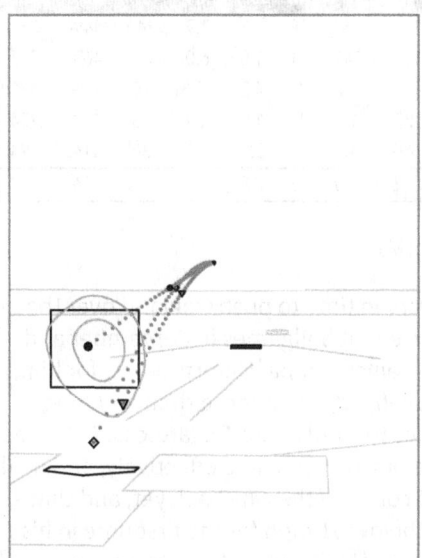

Pitch Shape vs RHH

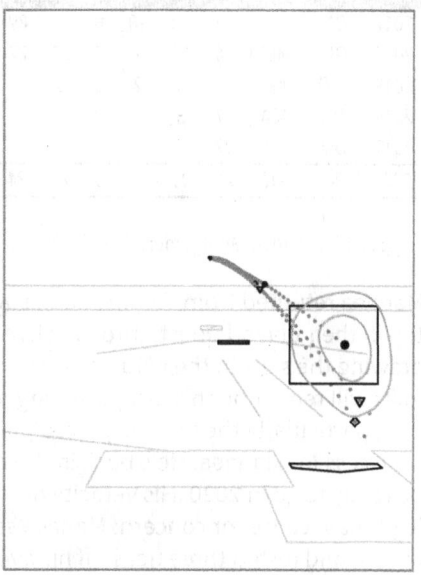

Type	Frequency	Velocity	H Movement	V Movement
● Fastball	67.8%	96.9 [113]	-4.7 [110]	-9.8 [116]
☐ Sinker				
+ Cutter				
▲ Changeup				
✕ Splitter				
▽ Slider	21.4%	89 [119]	2.7 [90]	-26.7 [118]
◇ Curveball	7.9%	84.8 [121]	3.2 [83]	-43.2 [109]
⊕ Slow Curveball				
✶ Knuckleball				
▼ Screwball				

Oakland Athletics 2020

Sean Manaea LHP

Born: 02/01/92   Age: 28   Bats: R   Throws: L
Height: 6'5"   Weight: 245   Origin: Round 1, 2013 Draft (#34 overall)

YEAR	TEAM	LVL	AGE	W	L	SV	G	GS	IP	H	HR	BB/9	K/9	K	GB%	BABIP
2017	OAK	MLB	25	12	10	0	29	29	158^2	167	18	3.1	7.9	140	44%	.318
2018	OAK	MLB	26	12	9	0	27	27	160^2	141	21	1.8	6.0	108	46%	.247
2019	STO	A+	27	0	2	0	3	3	8^1	14	1	4.3	10.8	10	43%	.481
2019	LVG	AAA	27	3	1	0	5	5	28	16	5	1.9	13.8	43	48%	.224
2019	OAK	MLB	27	4	0	0	5	5	29^2	16	3	2.1	9.1	30	41%	.194
2020	OAK	MLB	28	10	7	0	24	24	146	134	23	2.8	8.2	133	42%	.274

Comparables: Jordan Montgomery, Tyler Duffey, Steven Matz

Manaea returned from Tommy John surgery in time to push Oakland over the top in their playoff quest, throwing five excellent ballgames in September and drawing the start in the Wild Card round against Tampa. Unfortunately for him, folks will remember his disappointing playoff outing far more than anything else, particularly the two misplaced pitches to Yandy Díaz. Regardless, 2019 was a success for Manaea. He's back in the majors, he's pitching effectively, and he'll be ready to go in 2020. His velocity hasn't come *all* the way back yet, and that's legitimate cause for concern: Manaea sat below 91 mph for the first time in his career, and rested three ticks off his average velocity when he entered the league. September proved he could succeed without premium heat, but it was a five-start sample, with four coming against Detroit, Texas, and Seattle. If he can find that missing oomph, he could again be a solid No. 2/3 starter sooner rather than later.

YEAR	TEAM	LVL	AGE	WHIP	ERA	DRA	WARP	MPH	FB%	WHF	CSP
2017	OAK	MLB	25	1.40	4.37	5.17	0.7	94.1	58.3	12.1	46
2018	OAK	MLB	26	1.08	3.59	4.04	2.4	93.1	56.2	10.2	53.4
2019	STO	A+	27	2.16	9.72	9.37	-0.4				
2019	LVG	AAA	27	0.79	3.21	1.24	1.5				
2019	OAK	MLB	27	0.78	1.21	4.00	0.6	92.4	63.5	13.5	46.1
2020	OAK	MLB	28	1.23	3.87	4.20	2.2	92.8	58.2	11.4	48.8

Sean Manaea, continued

Pitch Shape vs LHH

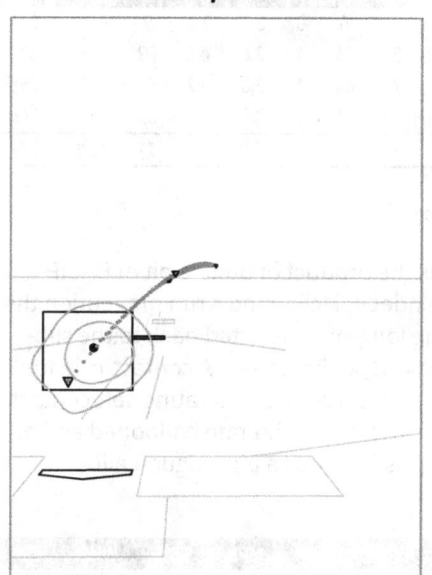

Pitch Shape vs RHH

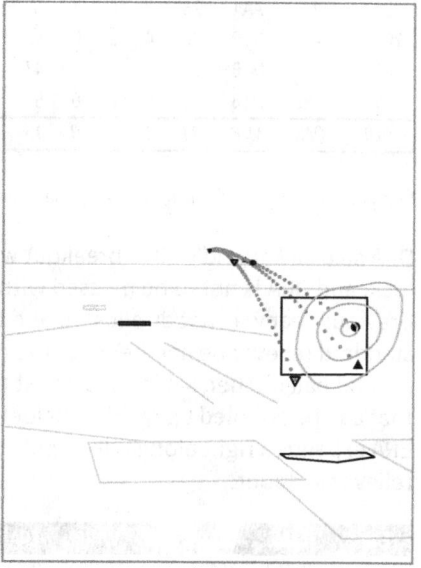

Type	Frequency	Velocity	H Movement	V Movement
● Fastball	63.5%	90.1 [94]	10.5 [84]	-20.4 [88]
☐ Sinker				
+ Cutter				
▲ Changeup	15.1%	81.3 [86]	10.8 [102]	-35.1 [77]
✕ Splitter				
▽ Slider	21.4%	79.6 [80]	-0.6 [82]	-38.6 [84]
◇ Curveball				
⊕ Slow Curveball				
✳ Knuckleball				
▼ Screwball				

T.J. McFarland LHP

Born: 06/08/89 Age: 31 Bats: L Throws: L
Height: 6'3" Weight: 220 Origin: Round 4, 2007 Draft (#137 overall)

YEAR	TEAM	LVL	AGE	W	L	SV	G	GS	IP	H	HR	BB/9	K/9	K	GB%	BABIP
2017	RNO	AAA	28	0	0	1	7	0	11	6	0	3.3	7.4	9	81%	.231
2017	ARI	MLB	28	4	5	0	43	1	54	65	4	2.8	4.8	29	69%	.323
2018	ARI	MLB	29	2	2	1	47	0	72	64	4	2.8	5.2	42	68%	.268
2019	ARI	MLB	30	0	0	0	51	0	56	71	6	3.2	5.6	35	62%	.346
2020	OAK	MLB	31	1	1	0	16	0	17	19	2	2.8	5.5	11	62%	.297

Comparables: Chris Rusin, Kyle Lobstein, Duane Below

DRA said McFarland's 2018 breakout was the product of quite a bit of BABIP luck, and DRA is not to be messed with. Indeed, McFarland's run prevention the previous year was not duplicated and the long-man reverted back to the sub-standard reliever he had been for the majority of his career. A contact-oriented, ground ball pitcher, McFarland's best path to success is generating soft contact that can be gobbled up by his infielders, but his hard-hit rate ballooned and his ERA expanded right alongside it, putting his future as a big league-caliber reliever in doubt.

YEAR	TEAM	LVL	AGE	WHIP	ERA	DRA	WARP	MPH	FB%	WHF	CSP
2017	RNO	AAA	28	0.91	0.00	2.90	0.3				
2017	ARI	MLB	28	1.52	5.33	5.89	-0.4	93.0	73.1	7.7	43.7
2018	ARI	MLB	29	1.19	2.00	4.72	0.2	92.1	72.7	8.8	41.6
2019	ARI	MLB	30	1.62	4.82	6.54	-0.7	90.8	68.6	10.8	42.8
2020	OAK	MLB	31	1.39	4.34	4.55	0.1	91.0	70.7	9.3	42.4

T.J. McFarland, continued

Pitch Shape vs LHH

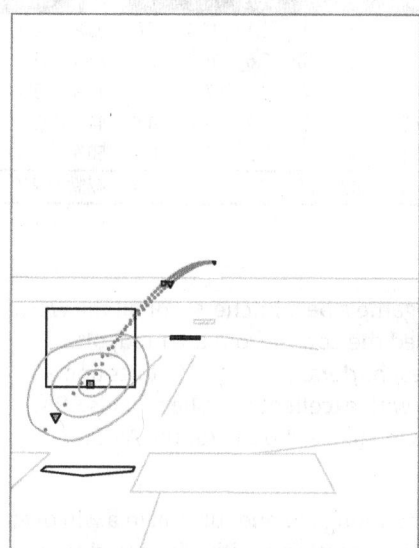

Pitch Shape vs RHH

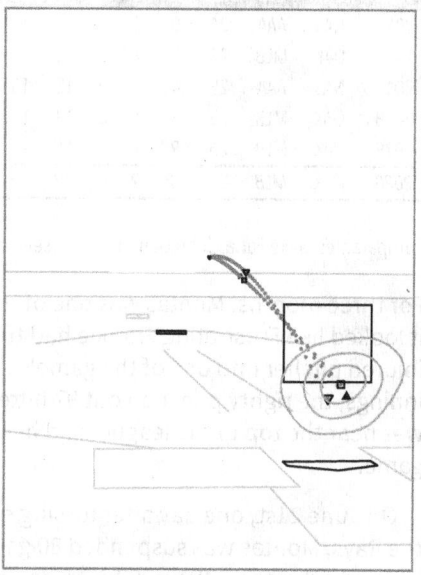

Type	Frequency	Velocity	H Movement	V Movement
● Fastball				
☐ Sinker	67.9%	89.5 [84]	15.2 [84]	-30.7 [64]
+ Cutter				
▲ Changeup	15.9%	82 [88]	14.2 [86]	-33.9 [81]
✕ Splitter				
▽ Slider	15.5%	81 [86]	-4.4 [97]	-39.6 [81]
◇ Curveball				
◈ Slow Curveball				
✱ Knuckleball				
▼ Screwball				

Oakland Athletics 2020

Frankie Montas RHP
Born: 03/21/93 Age: 27 Bats: R Throws: R
Height: 6'2" Weight: 245 Origin: International Free Agent, 2009

YEAR	TEAM	LVL	AGE	W	L	SV	G	GS	IP	H	HR	BB/9	K/9	K	GB%	BABIP
2017	NAS	AAA	24	0	2	0	9	8	29¹	25	4	2.1	11.4	37	53%	.296
2017	OAK	MLB	24	1	1	0	23	0	32	39	10	5.6	10.1	36	36%	.349
2018	NAS	AAA	25	4	5	0	15	15	71²	69	7	3.3	7.7	61	48%	.300
2018	OAK	MLB	25	5	4	0	13	11	65	74	5	2.9	6.0	43	44%	.325
2019	OAK	MLB	26	9	2	0	16	16	96	84	8	2.2	9.7	103	50%	.297
2020	OAK	MLB	27	12	9	0	29	29	175	163	22	3.3	9.3	181	47%	.299

Comparables: Jake Faria, John Gant, Robert Gsellman

For three months, Montas was one of the game's best pitchers. For all the world, it looked like Frustrating Frankie had turned the corner from talented, oft-injured pitcher into one of the game's finest hurlers. Through 15 starts and 90 innings, the righty punched out 97 hitters with excellent peripherals; his ERA was near the top of the league, and he looked like a shoe-in for the All-Star game.

On June 21st, one day after tossing eight innings of one run ball in a win over the Rays, Montas was suspended 80 games for testing positive for ostarine, a banned substance. News of his transgression struck like a thunderbolt, an uncomfortable flashback to the mid-aughts when we first learned to treat every breakout with cynical suspicion. Montas returned in September in time to make one final start, a good outing that did as much to highlight how much Oakland missed their ace in the one-game playoff as anything else. If there's a bright side here for Montas, it's that the baseball community has become much more tolerant of its PED users over time; Nelson Cruz's name is in better shape than many guys listed in the infamous Mitchell Report. If last year's breakout was real, and it's not clear why it wouldn't be, last year's suspension will soon become a footnote in his career.

YEAR	TEAM	LVL	AGE	WHIP	ERA	DRA	WARP	MPH	FB%	WHF	CSP
2017	NAS	AAA	24	1.09	5.22	2.53	1.0				
2017	OAK	MLB	24	1.84	7.03	6.69	-0.5	100.6	66.3	12.3	49.9
2018	NAS	AAA	25	1.33	4.65	4.42	0.9				
2018	OAK	MLB	25	1.46	3.88	5.59	-0.2	98.1	72.5	9.4	51.3
2019	OAK	MLB	26	1.11	2.62	3.16	2.7	98.9	56.8	12.7	49.3
2020	OAK	MLB	27	1.30	3.84	4.11	2.8	98.4	63.6	11.8	50.7

Frankie Montas, continued

Pitch Shape vs LHH

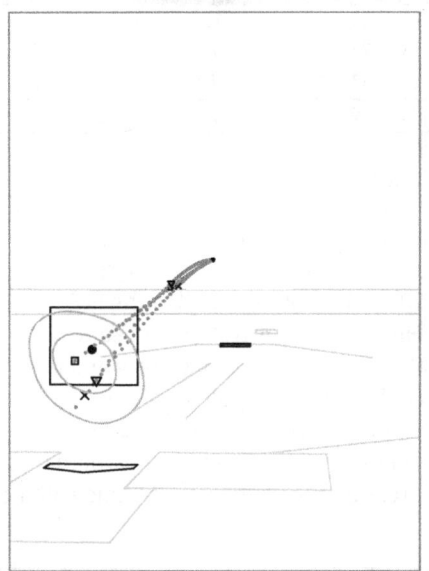

Pitch Shape vs RHH

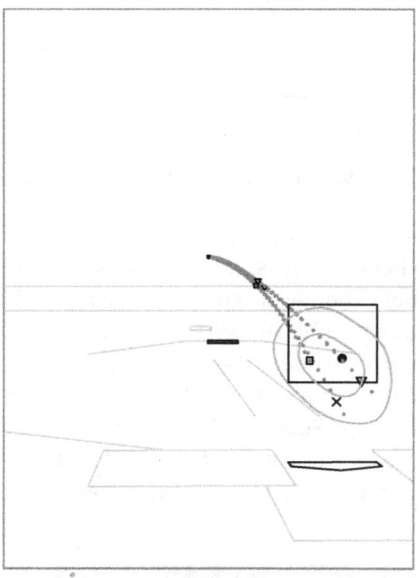

Type	Frequency	Velocity	H Movement	V Movement
● Fastball	17.9%	97.2 [114]	-7.4 [98]	-10.9 [113]
□ Sinker	38.9%	96.8 [122]	-13.7 [93]	-15.2 [118]
+ Cutter				
▲ Changeup				
× Splitter	18.3%	87.2 [109]	-10.7 [90]	-28.1 [104]
▽ Slider	24.9%	88.8 [119]	4.9 [100]	-27.5 [116]
◇ Curveball				
⊕ Slow Curveball				
✳ Knuckleball				
▼ Screwball				

Athletics Player Analysis - 61

Oakland Athletics 2020

Yusmeiro Petit   RHP

Born: 11/22/84   Age: 35   Bats: R   Throws: R
Height: 6'1"   Weight: 255   Origin: International Free Agent, 2001

YEAR	TEAM	LVL	AGE	W	L	SV	G	GS	IP	H	HR	BB/9	K/9	K	GB%	BABIP
2017	LAA	MLB	32	5	2	4	60	1	91¹	69	9	1.8	10.0	101	34%	.267
2018	OAK	MLB	33	7	3	0	74	0	93	76	13	1.7	7.4	76	36%	.241
2019	OAK	MLB	34	5	3	0	80	0	83	57	11	1.1	7.7	71	32%	.213
2020	OAK	MLB	35	3	3	2	60	0	63	59	13	1.9	7.9	56	33%	.266

Comparables: Dan Wheeler, Tim Stauffer, Brandon McCarthy

Petit is a righty with an 88 mph fastball, extremely low spin rates and... (double-checks notes) solid whiff rates and elite contact management numbers? This is not generally a skillset that plays well in 2019. But Petit does all of the little things right: His arm slot is a little funky. He has elite control. He's sneaky fast. While he doesn't get much spin on the ball, his hook moves like crazy and his change flops off the deck on its way to the plate. This may all be witchcraft: perhaps Petit has the ability to freeze time and uses his power to subtly tweak the location and trajectory of his pitches on their way to the plate. It would be a questionable use of such powers, to be sure, but one we're lucky to enjoy all the same.

YEAR	TEAM	LVL	AGE	WHIP	ERA	DRA	WARP	MPH	FB%	WHF	CSP
2017	LAA	MLB	32	0.95	2.76	2.83	2.4	91.4	47.8	11.6	48.5
2018	OAK	MLB	33	1.01	3.00	3.74	1.3	91.4	47.5	10	51.1
2019	OAK	MLB	34	0.81	2.71	3.93	1.3	90.8	45.8	12.4	49
2020	OAK	MLB	35	1.14	3.80	4.29	0.6	90.0	46.1	11.1	48.7

Yusmeiro Petit, continued

Pitch Shape vs LHH

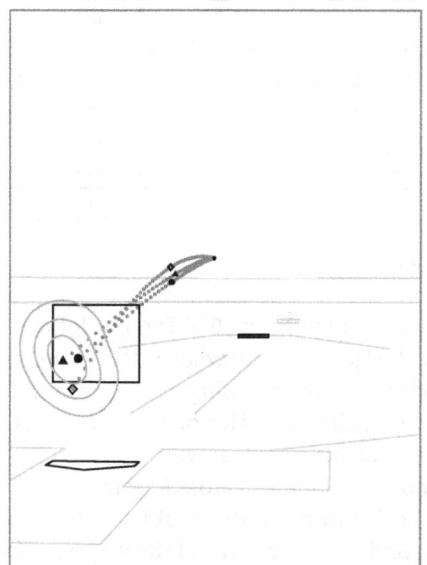

Pitch Shape vs RHH

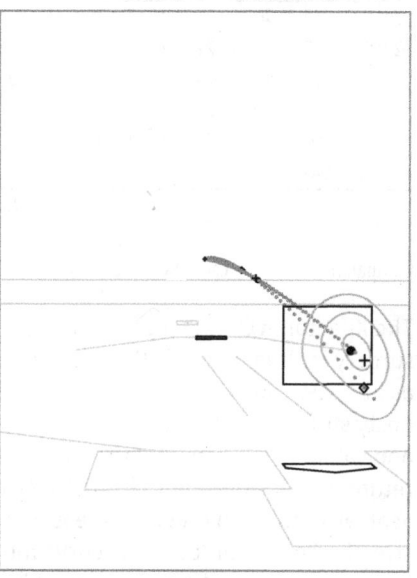

Type	Frequency	Velocity	H Movement	V Movement
● Fastball	45.8%	89.6 [92]	-5.1 [108]	-14.9 [103]
☐ Sinker				
+ Cutter	20.6%	85.9 [82]	-0.5 [86]	-18.8 [120]
▲ Changeup	19.4%	82 [88]	-8.6 [112]	-22.3 [115]
✕ Splitter				
▽ Slider				
◇ Curveball	14.3%	76.7 [94]	11.2 [115]	-39 [118]
⊕ Slow Curveball				
✳ Knuckleball				
▼ Screwball				

Athletics Player Analysis - 63

A.J. Puk LHP

Born: 04/25/95 Age: 25 Bats: L Throws: L
Height: 6'7" Weight: 238 Origin: Round 1, 2016 Draft (#6 overall)

YEAR	TEAM	LVL	AGE	W	L	SV	G	GS	IP	H	HR	BB/9	K/9	K	GB%	BABIP
2017	STO	A+	22	4	5	0	14	11	61	44	1	3.4	14.5	98	42%	.336
2017	MID	AA	22	2	5	0	13	13	64	64	2	3.5	12.1	86	48%	.380
2019	STO	A+	24	0	0	0	3	3	6	5	2	6.0	13.5	9	33%	.300
2019	MID	AA	24	0	0	0	6	1	8^1	9	2	3.2	14.0	13	58%	.412
2019	LVG	AAA	24	4	1	0	9	0	11	7	3	2.5	13.1	16	45%	.222
2019	OAK	MLB	24	2	0	0	10	0	11^1	10	1	4.0	10.3	13	45%	.321
2020	OAK	MLB	25	7	6	0	43	16	110	97	17	3.3	10.4	127	44%	.292

Comparables: José De León, Sean Newcomb, Brian Matusz

The X-factor in Oakland's farm system, Puk returned from 2018 Tommy John surgery in time to fortify the A's bullpen in September. And what a debut it was, as he struck out 13 hitters in 11 very effective innings, showing off legitimately nasty stuff along the way. He missed bats with all three of his primary offerings, and sat above 97 mph with the fastball. It's not entirely clear whether he's returned to his pre-injury form: He threw only 36 innings across four levels last year, all of them in relief or at least very short starting stints. He still needs to get stretched out, didn't use the curve much, and he may not be all the way past the lingering command problems most TJ returnees have to battle through. But anyone worried about his long term future after the surgery has to be encouraged at this point. Puk is again one of the game's top pitching prospects and he should challenge for big league starts right out of the chute.

YEAR	TEAM	LVL	AGE	WHIP	ERA	DRA	WARP	MPH	FB%	WHF	CSP
2017	STO	A+	22	1.10	3.69	2.35	2.0				
2017	MID	AA	22	1.39	4.36	3.51	1.3				
2019	STO	A+	24	1.50	6.00	5.31	0.0				
2019	MID	AA	24	1.44	4.32	5.92	-0.1				
2019	LVG	AAA	24	0.91	4.91	2.25	0.4				
2019	OAK	MLB	24	1.32	3.18	3.44	0.2	99.2	63.9	14.4	52.1
2020	OAK	MLB	25	1.25	3.79	4.11	1.7	98.9	65.4	14.7	53.4

A.J. Puk, continued

Pitch Shape vs LHH

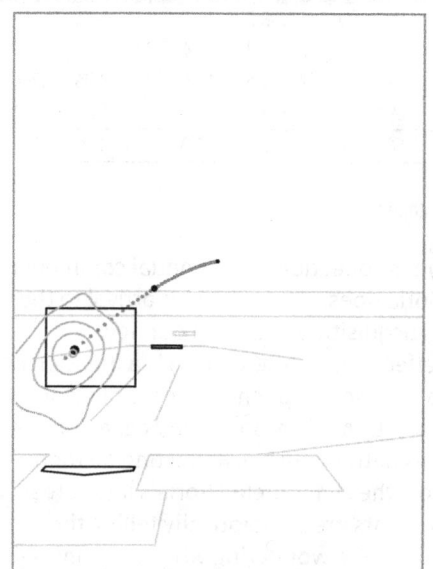

Pitch Shape vs RHH

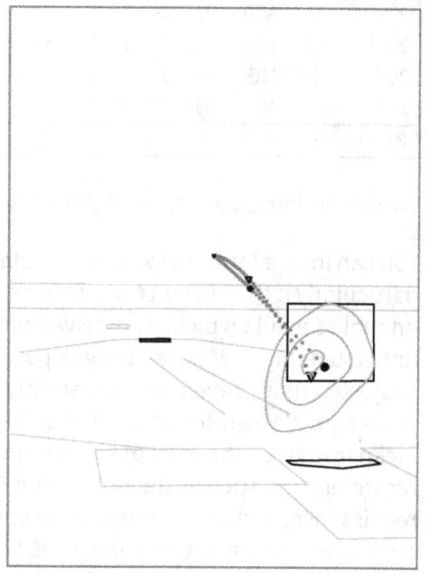

Type	Frequency	Velocity	H Movement	V Movement
● Fastball	63.9%	97.5 [115]	9.5 [88]	-12.7 [108]
☐ Sinker				
+ Cutter				
▲ Changeup	9.4%	89.8 [117]	12.6 [93]	-23.5 [111]
✕ Splitter				
▽ Slider	24.8%	90 [124]	-2 [88]	-25.6 [122]
◇ Curveball				
⬥ Slow Curveball				
✳ Knuckleball				
▼ Screwball				

Joakim Soria   RHP

Born: 05/18/84   Age: 36   Bats: R   Throws: R
Height: 6'3"   Weight: 200   Origin: International Free Agent, 2001

YEAR	TEAM	LVL	AGE	W	L	SV	G	GS	IP	H	HR	BB/9	K/9	K	GB%	BABIP
2017	KCA	MLB	33	4	3	1	59	0	56	49	1	3.2	10.3	64	58%	.329
2018	CHA	MLB	34	0	3	16	40	0	38^2	35	2	2.3	11.4	49	35%	.324
2018	MIL	MLB	34	3	1	0	26	0	22	18	2	2.5	10.6	26	48%	.286
2019	OAK	MLB	35	2	4	1	71	1	69	51	9	2.6	10.3	79	39%	.251
2020	OAK	MLB	36	3	3	4	55	0	58	50	8	2.7	10.0	64	41%	.285

Comparables: Luke Gregerson, John Wetteland, Jonathan Papelbon

You can infer a lot from looking at a player's collection of BP Annual comments, particularly if they have 14 of them, as Soria does. He marked his arrival to the Annual as a Rule 5 pick, a perceived nifty acquisition based on our new understanding of Mexican League park effects. From there, there's a mention of "adjusted runs prevented," apparently a proprietary pitching metric of some years ago. We also see a mention of "Mexicutioner" before Soria begged off the nickname given the level of violence in his native country. Reflecting on more recent entries, such as the note about how the slider fueled Soria's late career renaissance, and you see that these comments are symbiotically telling the story of a player and the game itself. So, if you're wondering why you found this book in the anthropology section, well, here's your answer.

YEAR	TEAM	LVL	AGE	WHIP	ERA	DRA	WARP	MPH	FB%	WHF	CSP
2017	KCA	MLB	33	1.23	3.70	3.62	1.0	95.1	49.3	13.5	46.6
2018	CHA	MLB	34	1.16	2.56	2.35	1.1	94.5	63	15.4	45.8
2018	MIL	MLB	34	1.09	4.09	2.94	0.5	94.8	71.2	14.2	50.1
2019	OAK	MLB	35	1.03	4.30	3.48	1.4	94.9	68.2	14.1	51.3
2020	OAK	MLB	36	1.16	3.28	3.64	1.0	93.5	61.7	13.9	47.8

Joakim Soria, continued

Pitch Shape vs LHH

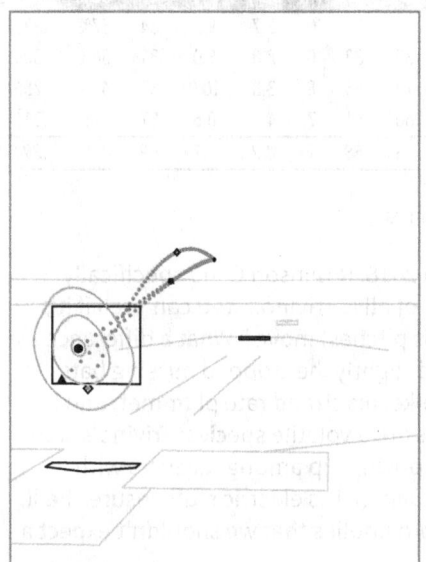

Pitch Shape vs RHH

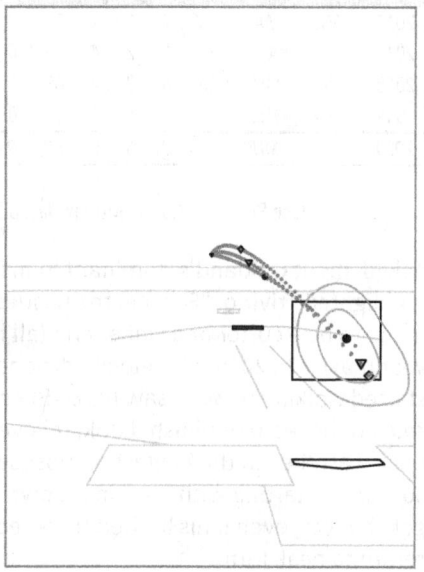

Type	Frequency	Velocity	H Movement	V Movement
● Fastball	67.0%	93.1 [102]	-4.3 [111]	-13.6 [106]
☐ Sinker				
+ Cutter				
▲ Changeup	6.9%	88 [110]	-8.9 [111]	-25.2 [106]
✕ Splitter				
▽ Slider	12.0%	81.8 [89]	12.4 [131]	-39.1 [83]
◇ Curveball	12.8%	73.5 [83]	15.2 [131]	-60.3 [73]
⊕ Slow Curveball				
✳ Knuckleball				
▼ Screwball				

Oakland Athletics 2020

Lou Trivino RHP

Born: 10/01/91   Age: 28   Bats: R   Throws: R
Height: 6'5"   Weight: 240   Origin: Round 11, 2013 Draft (#341 overall)

YEAR	TEAM	LVL	AGE	W	L	SV	G	GS	IP	H	HR	BB/9	K/9	K	GB%	BABIP
2017	MID	AA	25	7	1	1	23	0	33^1	31	0	2.7	9.2	34	57%	.333
2017	NAS	AAA	25	1	2	4	25	0	35	33	0	2.8	8.0	31	54%	.308
2018	OAK	MLB	26	8	3	4	69	1	74	53	8	3.8	10.0	82	47%	.256
2019	OAK	MLB	27	4	6	0	61	0	60	61	7	4.7	8.6	57	47%	.316
2020	OAK	MLB	28	3	3	0	60	0	63	58	9	4.2	9.7	69	46%	.294

Comparables: Josh Roenicke, Colton Murray, Jacob Barnes

Asked about Oakland's dominant 'pen in 2018, Robinson Canó specifically highlighted Trivino: "For me, the nastiest of all is Trivino... You can't tell if it's going to be a cutter or a sinker and (all his pitches) move." What a difference a year makes. In 2019, his velocity dropped slightly, he stopped missing bats, started walking people, saw his BABIP spike, his strand rate plummet, and his role on the team diminish. Look, relievers are a volatile species: Trivino's step back wasn't even the biggest or most surprising dip among relievers with surnames starting with "T-r" in his own bullpen. His electric stuff ensures he'll get chances, even if his limited track record implies that we shouldn't expect a return to peak form.

YEAR	TEAM	LVL	AGE	WHIP	ERA	DRA	WARP	MPH	FB%	WHF	CSP
2017	MID	AA	25	1.23	2.43	3.92	0.3				
2017	NAS	AAA	25	1.26	3.60	3.10	0.8				
2018	OAK	MLB	26	1.14	2.92	3.10	1.6	99.4	53.7	15.1	47.8
2019	OAK	MLB	27	1.53	5.25	4.67	0.4	98.9	50.8	13.3	46.3
2020	OAK	MLB	28	1.37	4.21	4.34	0.6	98.6	52.5	14.3	47.3

Lou Trivino, continued

Pitch Shape vs LHH

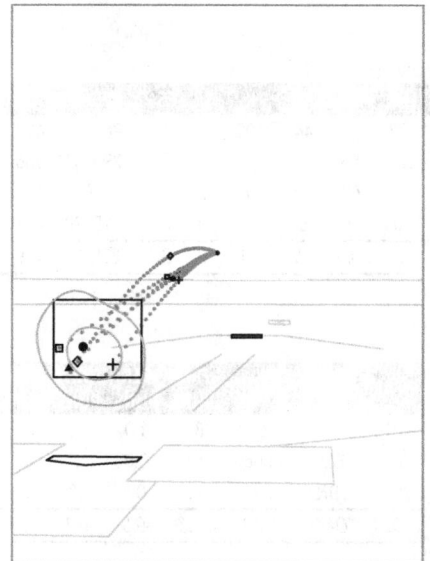

Pitch Shape vs RHH

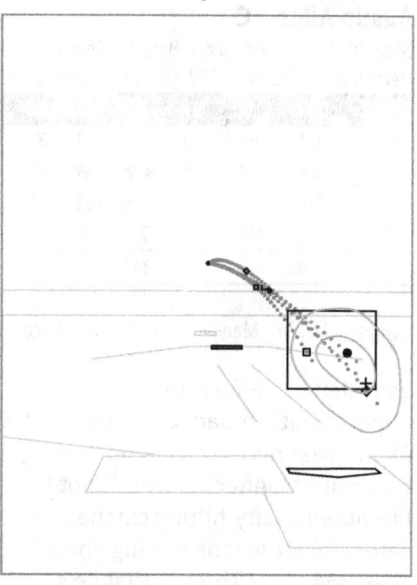

Type	Frequency	Velocity	H Movement	V Movement
● Fastball	34.0%	97.8 [115]	-7.9 [95]	-13.1 [108]
□ Sinker	16.8%	97.8 [127]	-13.3 [96]	-16.9 [112]
+ Cutter	33.9%	92.5 [124]	1.2 [96]	-21.9 [108]
▲ Changeup	4.8%	87.9 [110]	-14 [87]	-28.6 [97]
× Splitter				
▽ Slider				
◇ Curveball	10.5%	80.2 [105]	11.7 [117]	-45.7 [104]
⊕ Slow Curveball				
✽ Knuckleball				
▼ Screwball				

PLAYER COMMENTS WITHOUT GRAPHS

Austin Allen C
Born: 01/16/94 Age: 26 Bats: L Throws: R
Height: 6'2" Weight: 220 Origin: Round 4, 2015 Draft (#117 overall)

YEAR	TEAM	LVL	AGE	PA	R	2B	3B	HR	RBI	BB	K	SB	CS	AVG/OBP/SLG
2017	LEL	A+	23	516	71	31	1	22	81	44	109	0	1	.283/.353/.497
2018	SAN	AA	24	498	59	31	0	22	56	37	97	0	3	.290/.351/.506
2019	ELP	AAA	25	298	52	27	0	21	67	22	56	0	0	.330/.379/.663
2019	SDN	MLB	25	71	4	4	0	0	3	6	21	0	0	.215/.282/.277
2020	OAK	MLB	26	245	27	10	0	10	32	15	64	0	0	.238/.292/.419

Comparables: Trey Mancini, Ryan Cordell, Bruce Maxwell

Joan Jett can afford not to give a damn about her bad reputation, but in Allen's case his may wind up costing him millions. After all, what's not to like about a lefty-hitting catcher with a career minor-league batting line of .296/.354/.490? The fact that he's

YEAR	TEAM	P. COUNT	FRM RUNS	BLK RUNS	THRW RUNS	TOT RUNS
2018	SAN	12612	8.3	1.0	3.0	12.0
2019	ELP	8806	6.9	0.0	-1.2	5.5
2019	SDN	2293	-0.1	-0.4	0.0	-0.5
2020	OAK	9269	-0.3	-0.5	-0.1	-0.9

considered a lefty-hitting "catcher," that's what. The scare quotes come courtesy of scouts who have long questioned Allen's abilities behind the dish, a reputation that the young slugger certainly earned but has worked hard to change, without getting much traction. Despite showing well in our framing, blocking and overall fielding metrics over his last two seasons in the high minors, Allen is still branded a Doumit-class catcher/DH rather than a Pierzynski-class bat-first receiver. Given a fair shot, he'd likely zoom past the collective .237/.308/.406 line posted by big-league catchers last year, and with even sub-par defense Allen would be an improvement for many teams.

YEAR	TEAM	LVL	AGE	PA	DRC+	VORP	BABIP	BRR	FRAA	WARP
2017	LEL	A+	23	516	139	31.0	.326	-5.5	C(85): -5.4, 1B(1): 0.0	2.8
2018	SAN	AA	24	498	142	34.8	.325	-2.1	C(91): 14.6, 1B(19): -1.5	5.2
2019	ELP	AAA	25	298	128	25.1	.345	-2.5	C(60): 7.2, 1B(2): -0.1	2.8
2019	SDN	MLB	25	71	62	-0.1	.318	0.0	C(19): -0.2, 1B(2): 0.1	0.0
2020	OAK	MLB	26	245	90	7.8	.286	-0.5	C 0	0.8

Nick Allen SS

Born: 10/08/98 Age: 21 Bats: R Throws: R
Height: 5'9" Weight: 166 Origin: Round 3, 2017 Draft (#81 overall)

YEAR	TEAM	LVL	AGE	PA	R	2B	3B	HR	RBI	BB	K	SB	CS	AVG/OBP/SLG
2017	ATH	RK	18	154	26	3	2	1	14	13	28	7	3	.254/.322/.326
2018	BLT	A	19	512	51	17	6	0	34	34	85	24	8	.239/.301/.302
2019	STO	A+	20	328	45	22	5	3	25	28	52	13	5	.292/.363/.434
2020	OAK	MLB	21	251	20	11	1	3	21	15	56	5	2	.222/.277/.319

Comparables: Ehire Adrianza, Tyler Wade, Jose Pirela

Allen took a step forward last year, which is something to savor now because you won't be reading many more happy stories from this farm system. Already one of the best defenders in the minors, Allen had a surprisingly productive year at the plate. He hit nearly .300 as a 20-year-old in the Cal League, with respectable plate discipline and even a few homers. Scouts are still concerned that advanced pitchers will knock the bat out of his hands, but he looks more likely to crack a big-league lineup now than he did at this time last year. If he can, the A's will have a good player on their hands, because Allen is the total package at shortstop. He has above-average range, a plus arm, good instincts, and excellent hands. He'll have no trouble staying at the position, and he could be a 70 defender at maturity. Don't be too concerned if he struggles at Double-A in 2020: he's moving fast and is ahead of schedule.

YEAR	TEAM	LVL	AGE	PA	DRC+	VORP	BABIP	BRR	FRAA	WARP
2017	ATH	RK	18	154	99	6.8	.312	1.1	SS(33): 2.5	1.0
2018	BLT	A	19	512	74	15.2	.289	3.7	SS(121): 5.2	1.8
2019	STO	A+	20	328	135	17.6	.348	-4.4	SS(45): 4.7, 2B(24): -1.6	2.1
2020	OAK	MLB	21	251	60	-5.0	.281	0.2	SS 3, 2B 0	-0.2

Oakland Athletics 2020

Lazaro Armenteros OF

Born: 05/22/99   Age: 21   Bats: R   Throws: R
Height: 6'0"   Weight: 182   Origin: International Free Agent, 2016

YEAR	TEAM	LVL	AGE	PA	R	2B	3B	HR	RBI	BB	K	SB	CS	AVG/OBP/SLG
2017	DAT	RK	18	26	6	0	0	0	1	3	9	2	2	.167/.385/.167
2017	ATH	RK	18	181	24	9	4	4	22	16	48	10	1	.288/.376/.474
2018	BLT	A	19	340	43	8	2	8	39	36	115	8	6	.277/.374/.401
2019	STO	A+	20	538	65	22	5	17	61	73	227	22	6	.222/.336/.403
2020	OAK	MLB	21	251	20	10	1	4	21	19	113	2	1	.191/.264/.295

Comparables: Tyler O'Neill, Ryan McMahon, Nick Williams

Armenteros is a tooled-up 20-year-old from Cuba with obvious raw power, good speed, and a 25 percent whiff rate in the soft toss drill. Pedro Serrano comps fly thick and fast around this type of player, but in Armenteros, we may have found a case where it's unfair *to Serrano*. A big hack, poor pitch recognition and an utter inability to hit bendy things neutralized a man who did plenty of damage when he did connect. He hit 17 bombs and was actually a tick better than league average at the plate—not too shabby at his age in High-A. Still, even as a youngin', even in this boom-or-bust era of baseball, you can't strike out 42 percent of the time and project as a big leaguer. The tools are tantalizing, but short of an intervention from Jobu, he'll get carved by upper-level arms.

YEAR	TEAM	LVL	AGE	PA	DRC+	VORP	BABIP	BRR	FRAA	WARP
2017	DAT	RK	18	26	39	1.8	.300	0.9	CF(6): 1.5	0.2
2017	ATH	RK	18	181	110	14.5	.387	2.8	LF(28): 4.2, CF(2): -0.5	1.1
2018	BLT	A	19	340	121	21.6	.427	2.1	LF(69): -0.7	1.6
2019	STO	A+	20	538	102	18.0	.395	2.4	LF(112): -1.3, CF(7): -0.1	1.4
2020	OAK	MLB	21	251	49	-8.5	.357	0.0	LF 1, CF 0	-0.7

Austin Beck CF

Born: 11/21/98 Age: 21 Bats: R Throws: R
Height: 6'1" Weight: 200 Origin: Round 1, 2017 Draft (#6 overall)

YEAR	TEAM	LVL	AGE	PA	R	2B	3B	HR	RBI	BB	K	SB	CS	AVG/OBP/SLG
2017	ATH	RK	18	174	23	7	4	2	28	17	51	7	1	.211/.293/.349
2018	BLT	A	19	534	58	29	4	2	60	30	117	8	6	.296/.335/.383
2019	STO	A+	20	367	40	22	4	8	49	24	126	2	2	.251/.302/.411
2020	OAK	MLB	21	251	20	12	1	3	22	16	95	1	1	.216/.270/.324

Comparables: Willy García, Trayvon Robinson, Gabriel Guerrero

More than most teams, the A's draft for upside. Sometimes that gamble lands you Sonny Gray; sometimes your first-rounder quits to play football instead. Beck, Oakland's top pick in 2017, fits the general pattern. As an amateur, a knee injury initially kept him below the radar as a draft prospect, but his stock surged when he finally got healthy and terrorized overmatched North Carolina high schoolers as a senior. There's plenty of risk in any late-bloomer, but with huge bat speed and an athletic, powerful frame, Beck offered enticing potential in a draft largely lacking it.

Two-and-a-half years later though, the selection seems like a reach. Beck had a bumpy transition to pro ball, and the 20-year-old has yet to hit for power in games. There's plenty of time for things to turn around, and this profile—toolsy, light amateur resume—is often a slow burn. As it is though, Beck was a below-average hitter in the Cal League last summer and he's probably more of a corner guy than a center fielder. He needs a big 2020 to avoid the dreaded tweener label.

YEAR	TEAM	LVL	AGE	PA	DRC+	VORP	BABIP	BRR	FRAA	WARP
2017	ATH	RK	18	174	59	2.7	.294	1.8	CF(33): 1.2	0.2
2018	BLT	A	19	534	105	14.9	.377	-4.8	CF(113): 2.0	1.6
2019	STO	A+	20	367	92	7.5	.372	-0.1	CF(69): -0.3, RF(10): 2.7	1.1
2020	OAK	MLB	21	251	57	-6.2	.347	-0.3	CF -2, RF 0	-0.8

Oakland Athletics 2020

Marcos Brito SS
Born: 03/06/00   Age: 20   Bats: B   Throws: R
Height: 6'0"   Weight: 165   Origin: International Free Agent, 2016

YEAR	TEAM	LVL	AGE	PA	R	2B	3B	HR	RBI	BB	K	SB	CS	AVG/OBP/SLG
2017	DAT	RK	17	62	3	1	0	0	8	13	8	5	0	.178/.339/.200
2017	ATH	RK	17	194	30	4	2	1	17	21	42	4	1	.234/.320/.298
2018	VER	A-	18	241	29	5	1	1	20	27	50	7	6	.241/.325/.288
2019	BLT	A	19	228	21	8	0	2	13	22	67	3	4	.181/.260/.250
2020	OAK	MLB	20	251	20	10	1	3	20	24	82	2	1	.199/.279/.289

Comparables: Deivy Grullon, Willi Castro, Juniel Querecuto

Billed as a second baseman who could hit, Brito was signed out of the Dominican Republic for $1.1 million back in 2016. Three years later, he's still a second baseman but he hasn't fulfilled the second part of the bargain. The switch-hitter struggled badly in 2019: He didn't hit lefties, didn't hit righties, didn't hit for power and, well, looking at the strikeout totals, it doesn't appear he hit much of anything at all. Brito won't turn 20 until Spring Training, so he has time to turn things around, but he was overmatched in A-ball and it's a long row to hoe from there.

YEAR	TEAM	LVL	AGE	PA	DRC+	VORP	BABIP	BRR	FRAA	WARP
2017	DAT	RK	17	62	134	1.7	.195	0.3	2B(6): -0.6, SS(5): -0.9	0.2
2017	ATH	RK	17	194	64	0.2	.302	1.2	2B(34): -4.9, SS(5): -1.0	-0.5
2018	VER	A-	18	241	108	-0.9	.309	-3.6	2B(52): -0.6, SS(1): -0.4	0.4
2019	BLT	A	19	228	62	-4.1	.257	0.6	SS(60): -7.6	-0.7
2020	OAK	MLB	20	251	55	-6.9	.297	-0.2	2B -1, SS -2	-1.0

Logan Davidson SS

Born: 12/26/97 Age: 22 Bats: B Throws: R
Height: 6'3" Weight: 185 Origin: Round 1, 2019 Draft (#29 overall)

YEAR	TEAM	LVL	AGE	PA	R	2B	3B	HR	RBI	BB	K	SB	CS	AVG/OBP/SLG
2019	VER	A-	21	238	42	7	0	4	12	31	55	5	0	.239/.345/.332
2020	OAK	MLB	22	251	22	11	0	5	24	16	80	2	1	.214/.268/.333

Comparables: Tyler Greene, Taylor Featherston, Trea Turner

Oakland's first-round pick last summer, Davidson is a modern, bat-first shortstop. At 6-foot-3, he's a big guy for the position, and both his arm and range suggest that he'll be competent, if not exactly Gold Glove material at the six. If everything clicks at the plate though, he could bloom into a Silver Slugger candidate. Davidson is a switch-hitter with pop from both sides. There's a lot of swing and miss in his game, but he posted double-digit homer totals all three seasons at Clemson and he takes his share of walks too. There's 25-homer upside in the bat, and if he hits enough of those, probably an average or better hit tool to go with them. He acquitted himself well enough in a pitcher-friendly short-season league after signing, and should be ready for High-A out of the gate in 2020.

YEAR	TEAM	LVL	AGE	PA	DRC+	VORP	BABIP	BRR	FRAA	WARP
2019	VER	A-	21	238	133	16.0	.308	1.5	SS(49): 11.8	3.0
2020	OAK	MLB	22	251	61	-4.6	.300	0.0	SS 4	-0.1

Oakland Athletics 2020

Jordan Diaz 3B

Born: 08/13/00   Age: 19   Bats: R   Throws: R
Height: 5'10"   Weight: 175   Origin: International Free Agent, 2016

YEAR	TEAM	LVL	AGE	PA	R	2B	3B	HR	RBI	BB	K	SB	CS	AVG/OBP/SLG
2017	ATH	RK	16	28	2	0	0	0	2	0	4	1	0	.185/.179/.185
2017	DAT	RK	16	149	14	7	0	0	18	6	22	2	0	.255/.295/.307
2018	ATH	RK	17	186	23	11	2	1	25	19	22	0	2	.277/.371/.390
2019	VER	A-	18	300	31	17	1	9	47	18	46	2	2	.264/.307/.430
2020	OAK	MLB	19	251	23	13	1	6	26	15	54	0	0	.226/.277/.362

Comparables: Maikel Franco, Eloy Jiménez, Harold Ramirez

Diaz has a bunch of 45s and 50s on the scouting report, but if he has upside, it's in the one area it matters. Just a teenager, Diaz took well to short-season ball, making plenty of contact and hitting for enough thump to suggest above-average power down the line if he leans into that part of his game. He'll need to hit, because he's just an okay third basemen and there aren't a whole lot of enticing secondary skills. Oakland farmhands have made a habit of crashing in the Midwest League recently, and the cold weather and jump in competition should challenge the Colombian in 2020. Should he pass the test, he'll be on our Top 10 A's prospects for 2021.

YEAR	TEAM	LVL	AGE	PA	DRC+	VORP	BABIP	BRR	FRAA	WARP
2017	ATH	RK	16	28	46	-2.0	.208	0.2	3B(8): -0.5	-0.1
2017	DAT	RK	16	149	93	0.9	.297	0.7	3B(33): 0.8, 3B(7): 0.8	0.5
2018	ATH	RK	17	186	147	10.7	.312	-0.9	3B(44): -2.5, 2B(1): 0.0	1.1
2019	VER	A-	18	300	144	16.8	.283	-0.9	3B(61): -2.5	1.7
2020	OAK	MLB	19	251	69	-2.5	.270	-0.4	3B -2, C 0	-0.4

Jeremy Eierman SS

Born: 09/10/96 Age: 23 Bats: R Throws: R
Height: 6'0" Weight: 205 Origin: Round 2, 2018 Draft (#70 overall)

YEAR	TEAM	LVL	AGE	PA	R	2B	3B	HR	RBI	BB	K	SB	CS	AVG/OBP/SLG
2018	VER	A-	21	267	36	8	2	8	26	13	70	10	4	.235/.283/.381
2019	STO	A+	22	552	57	22	7	13	64	39	177	11	3	.208/.270/.357
2020	OAK	MLB	23	251	23	11	1	8	27	15	95	4	2	.202/.254/.355

Comparables: Jaycob Brugman, Kevin Cron, Chase d'Arnaud

School teachers often offer a simple guideline in regards to books: You can put them down, but you should give one 25-30 pages first. Fortunately for Eierman, the same principle applies to early draftees. Eierman is a bat-first shortstop who needed to show he could rake in the Cal League last summer. Instead, he hit .208 with big strikeout totals and without enough thump to compensate. Even worse, he played about a third of his games at second or third. A weak stick with occasional pop is tolerable in a great gloveman or backup catcher, but unusable pretty much anywhere else. We're still only 20 pages into this story, but thus far it's not looking promising.

YEAR	TEAM	LVL	AGE	PA	DRC+	VORP	BABIP	BRR	FRAA	WARP
2018	VER	A-	21	267	74	5.6	.294	-0.1	SS(56): 0.3, 2B(2): 0.9	0.6
2019	STO	A+	22	552	68	11.5	.289	3.7	SS(90): -8.6, 2B(33): 1.1	0.1
2020	OAK	MLB	23	251	60	-5.0	.301	0.0	SS -2, 2B 0	-0.7

Jorge Mateo SS

Born: 06/23/95   Age: 25   Bats: R   Throws: R
Height: 6'0"   Weight: 192   Origin: International Free Agent, 2012

YEAR	TEAM	LVL	AGE	PA	R	2B	3B	HR	RBI	BB	K	SB	CS	AVG/OBP/SLG
2017	TAM	A+	22	297	39	16	8	4	11	16	79	28	3	.240/.288/.400
2017	TRN	AA	22	140	26	9	3	4	26	15	32	11	7	.300/.381/.525
2017	MID	AA	22	147	25	5	7	4	20	9	33	13	3	.292/.333/.518
2018	NAS	AAA	23	510	50	17	16	3	45	29	139	25	10	.230/.280/.353
2019	LVG	AAA	24	566	95	29	14	19	78	29	145	24	11	.289/.330/.504
2020	OAK	MLB	25	105	10	5	1	2	10	5	31	6	2	.228/.273/.372

Comparables: Abiatal Avelino, Andrew Velazquez, Yairo Muñoz

Mateo has long been a mercurial prospect, and at a glance, his numbers imply he made progress after a disappointing 2018 season. With Jorge though, surprises lurk at every turn. In this era of PCL baseball, a .289/.330/.504 slash line is below par; his slugging percentage was actually one of the lowest marks on the team. That leaves Mateo more or less where we found him this time last year. He's still the fastest guy on the field, but he strikes out too often, probably won't hit enough to make an impact and ultimately projects as a utility man.

YEAR	TEAM	LVL	AGE	PA	DRC+	VORP	BABIP	BRR	FRAA	WARP
2017	TAM	A+	22	297	87	15.6	.321	7.6	SS(42): 2.9, CF(22): -0.8	1.8
2017	TRN	AA	22	140	127	16.7	.372	1.6	SS(17): 1.1, CF(7): -0.4	1.3
2017	MID	AA	22	147	105	14.8	.356	2.2	SS(30): 0.8	1.0
2018	NAS	AAA	23	510	61	3.7	.316	1.1	SS(123): -0.8, 2B(4): -0.5	-0.1
2019	LVG	AAA	24	566	81	27.8	.366	3.2	SS(100): 16.6, 2B(14): -0.2	2.9
2020	OAK	MLB	25	105	68	0.2	.312	0.5	CF 0, 2B 0	0.1

Kyler Murray OF/QB
Born: 08/07/97   Age: 22   Bats: R   Throws: R
Height: 5'11"   Weight: 195   Origin: Round 1, 2018 Draft (#9 overall)

When asked "how can we jazz up baseball," the game's gatekeepers can't help but amend the question by tacking on "and how will it save us money?" When your only tool is a hammer and all that. Look, maybe Murray was always going to play football. He was a better prospect on the gridiron, and that seems to be where his heart lies. But money talks and baseball's push to muzzle signing bonuses has always been penny-wise, pound-stupid and this is the clearest example why. Murray is a unicorn, an athlete with crossover appeal who had the potential to attract eyeballs in a way that no current big leaguer possibly can. That player is insanely valuable to a league that cashed in most of its mainstream cultural appeal decades ago. Or, at least he should be. There's a cap on signing bonuses now, you know, and MLB just couldn't figure out how to raise the ceiling enough to change Murray's destiny without—gasp!—creating a precedent. In the end, the league saved a few bucks up front. I'm sure A's fans were delighted by the austerity; Arizona Cardinals fans sure are.

Oakland Athletics 2020

Robert Puason SS
Born: 09/11/02   Age: 17   Bats: B   Throws: R
Height: 6'3"   Weight: 165   Origin: International Free Agent, 2019

Puason was one of the top-rated J2 signees last summer, and the A's paid him more than $5 million to sign on the dotted line. If you have to buy a 16-year-old player, you might as well take the twitchy shortstop who can hit a ball nearly 400 feet. But for crying out loud, Puason is sixteen. The Latin American market has long been little more than an exploitative dart throw, and if you don't believe us about that last point, take a look at Baseball America's top prospects for the international signing period from 10 years ago. Miguel Sanó ranked first and Gary Sánchez featured two spots behind him—familiar, successful names. But sandwiched in between was Wagner Mateo, who became infamous in prospecting circles for having his signing bonus voided once the Cardinals discovered he had terrible eyesight. Later in the top 10, you'll find luminaries like Guillermo Pimentel, Juan Urbina, and Jose Sanchez. Puason looks like a nice player, but let's wait until he's an adult before we start speculating on his ceiling.

Tyler Baum RHP

Born: 01/14/98 Age: 22 Bats: R Throws: R
Height: 6'2" Weight: 195 Origin: Round 2, 2019 Draft (#66 overall)

YEAR	TEAM	LVL	AGE	W	L	SV	G	GS	IP	H	HR	BB/9	K/9	K	GB%	BABIP
2019	VER	A-	21	0	3	0	11	11	30^2	29	4	2.1	10.0	34	40%	.306
2020	OAK	MLB	22	2	2	0	33	0	35	35	6	3.3	8.0	31	38%	.294

Comparables: Joel Carreno, Pat Light, Jensen Lewis

With a low-90s fastball and a chance to have four average pitches, Baum spent most of his college career looking like a solid, if unspectacular, prospect—the kind usually ticketed for the fifth round. But humans tend to value small samples of exciting, recently absorbed information more favorably than a larger but older collection of less impressionable material. That worked in Baum's favor when a late-season velocity spike sent his fastball into the mid-90s and propelled him to a second-round selection. Whether that extra heat tangibly alters his career trajectory or was simply the baseball equivalent of pulling an all-nighter before the final will be for time and the Athletics player development staff to sort out.

YEAR	TEAM	LVL	AGE	WHIP	ERA	DRA	WARP	MPH	FB%	WHF	CSP
2019	VER	A-	21	1.17	4.70	4.42	0.3				
2020	OAK	MLB	22	1.38	4.66	4.82	0.1				

Parker Dunshee RHP

Born: 02/12/95 Age: 25 Bats: R Throws: R
Height: 6'0" Weight: 215 Origin: Round 7, 2017 Draft (#201 overall)

YEAR	TEAM	LVL	AGE	W	L	SV	G	GS	IP	H	HR	BB/9	K/9	K	GB%	BABIP
2017	VER	A-	22	1	0	0	12	9	38^1	15	0	1.9	10.6	45	46%	.185
2018	STO	A+	23	6	2	0	12	10	70	61	7	2.2	10.5	82	35%	.314
2018	MID	AA	23	7	4	0	12	12	80^2	59	5	1.6	9.0	81	34%	.266
2019	MID	AA	24	2	2	0	6	6	38	26	1	2.6	8.1	34	38%	.255
2019	LVG	AAA	24	4	5	1	20	19	92	86	21	3.6	8.8	90	35%	.261
2020	OAK	MLB	25	2	2	0	25	3	38	38	6	3.3	8.2	34	35%	.299

Comparables: Michael King, Brandon Workman, Erick Fedde

Twenty-four is roughly the age at which spending time in Las Vegas stops being any fun, as Dunshee himself discovered last summer. Sure, the glitz and the lights are novel at first, and the occasional free drink can make anyone feel like a VIP. In time though, everyone realizes that the decks are stacked the wrong way, the water tastes salty, the free gin and tonic actually costs forty bucks and the baseballs carry deep into the night. That last one particularly applies to our beleaguered right-hander. Dunshee's command-n-control, low-90s profile ran smack into the juiced ball and desert climes of the PCL, and the results were as ugly as hitting on 17. If you can look past the garishly flashy home run rate, there's a functional pitcher here, so long as he can clear the last Vegas obstacle: leaving.

YEAR	TEAM	LVL	AGE	WHIP	ERA	DRA	WARP	MPH	FB%	WHF	CSP
2017	VER	A-	22	0.60	0.00	1.86	1.5				
2018	STO	A+	23	1.11	2.70	3.03	1.8				
2018	MID	AA	23	0.90	2.01	2.47	2.7				
2019	MID	AA	24	0.97	1.89	3.29	0.8				
2019	LVG	AAA	24	1.34	5.38	3.64	2.7				
2020	OAK	MLB	25	1.39	4.79	4.97	0.2				

Daulton Jefferies RHP

Born: 08/02/95 Age: 24 Bats: L Throws: R
Height: 6'0" Weight: 182 Origin: Round 1, 2016 Draft (#37 overall)

YEAR	TEAM	LVL	AGE	W	L	SV	G	GS	IP	H	HR	BB/9	K/9	K	GB%	BABIP
2017	STO	A+	21	0	0	0	2	1	7	7	0	1.3	7.7	6	67%	.292
2019	STO	A+	23	1	0	0	5	3	15	10	1	1.2	12.6	21	44%	.273
2019	MID	AA	23	1	2	0	21	12	64	63	7	1.0	10.1	72	42%	.327
2020	OAK	MLB	24	1	1	0	22	0	23	23	3	3.0	9.4	24	40%	.308

Comparables: Michael King, Daniel Gossett, Brandon Workman

Jefferies has battled injury problems throughout his career—broken pitchers grow on oak trees—and the 64 innings he threw last summer account for the lion's share of his professional workload. Fortunately for all parties, Jefferies looked little worse for wear in his return from an extended absence. At his best, he combines an above-average fastball with a firm but effective change that projects as a plus offering. Those weapons were intact, albeit in short stints: His workload was spread across 21 outings and he never finished the fourth in any one game. Still, he managed to whiff more than a batter per inning across two levels, and looked sharp at Double-A. The A's will understandably try to stretch him out more next summer, but if the club ever decides the juice isn't quite worth the squeeze there, he would be very effective in short stints or a multi-inning relief role.

YEAR	TEAM	LVL	AGE	WHIP	ERA	DRA	WARP	MPH	FB%	WHF	CSP
2017	STO	A+	21	1.14	2.57	4.07	0.1				
2019	STO	A+	23	0.80	2.40	2.57	0.4				
2019	MID	AA	23	1.09	3.66	3.39	1.1				
2020	OAK	MLB	24	1.32	4.27	4.61	0.1				

James Kaprielian RHP

Born: 03/02/94 Age: 26 Bats: R Throws: R
Height: 6'3" Weight: 210 Origin: Round 1, 2015 Draft (#16 overall)

YEAR	TEAM	LVL	AGE	W	L	SV	G	GS	IP	H	HR	BB/9	K/9	K	GB%	BABIP
2019	STO	A+	25	2	2	0	11	10	36^1	35	6	2.0	10.7	43	32%	.319
2019	MID	AA	25	2	1	0	7	5	27^2	18	2	2.6	8.5	26	41%	.232
2020	OAK	MLB	26	3	3	0	32	5	52	51	8	3.1	8.7	50	39%	.301

Comparables: Joe Musgrove, Glenn Sparkman, David Phelps

There comes a time when a minor-league pitcher simply has too many injuries on the ledger to be taken seriously as a prospect. For Kaprielian, who battled flexor issues and then separately needed Tommy John surgery, that point may well have been three years ago. Just when all hope seemed lost, the right-hander turned in a pretty healthy season, though one that brought fresh concerns. At his peak Kaprelian had an electric arm, and between that and his injury history, it made all the sense in the world for Oakland to push him aggressively in 2019. So when the A's both played it safe—he averaged less than four innings per appearance—and opted not to promote him to the bigs for the stretch run, well, that and diminished velocity suggests the former second-rounder isn't all the way back. There's still upside here, but the No. 2 starter ceiling from draft day seems like a pipe dream.

YEAR	TEAM	LVL	AGE	WHIP	ERA	DRA	WARP	MPH	FB%	WHF	CSP
2019	STO	A+	25	1.18	4.46	4.47	0.2				
2019	MID	AA	25	0.94	1.63	3.01	0.6				
2020	OAK	MLB	26	1.34	4.46	4.71	0.4				

Jesus Luzardo LHP

Born: 09/30/97   Age: 22   Bats: L   Throws: L
Height: 6'0"   Weight: 209   Origin: Round 3, 2016 Draft (#94 overall)

YEAR	TEAM	LVL	AGE	W	L	SV	G	GS	IP	H	HR	BB/9	K/9	K	GB%	BABIP
2017	NAT	RK	19	1	0	0	3	3	13²	14	1	0.0	9.9	15	33%	.342
2017	ATH	RK	19	0	1	0	4	3	11²	9	0	0.8	10.0	13	58%	.290
2017	VER	A-	19	1	0	0	5	5	18	12	1	2.0	10.0	20	53%	.250
2018	STO	A+	20	2	1	0	3	3	14²	6	0	3.1	15.3	25	56%	.240
2018	MID	AA	20	7	3	0	16	16	78²	58	5	2.1	9.8	86	46%	.268
2018	NAS	AAA	20	1	1	0	4	4	16	25	2	3.9	10.1	18	51%	.469
2019	STO	A+	21	1	0	0	3	1	10	6	1	0.0	16.2	18	50%	.294
2019	LVG	AAA	21	1	1	0	7	7	31	29	3	2.3	9.9	34	56%	.302
2019	OAK	MLB	21	0	0	2	6	0	12	5	1	2.2	12.0	16	42%	.160
2020	OAK	MLB	22	9	7	0	43	21	128	109	18	3.7	11.0	156	48%	.294

Comparables: Luiz Gohara, Alex Reyes, Tyler Skaggs

If there are better pitching prospects than Luzardo, you wouldn't need more than five fingers to count them. In many ways, he's the Platonic ideal of what a pitching prospect should look like. He's 22, athletic, left-handed, throws 100 mph and he misses bats with both a sharp curve and a delightful fading changeup. The ingredients are great, but Luzardo is also very polished for someone so young and naturally gifted. He can move the ball around the zone, and is able to attack both lefties and righties with his curve. He even generates ground balls: The two-seamer may be falling out of fashion, but if yours sits in the high-90s with vicious tail, you can still chew threw a lot of bats pretty quickly. If there's a concern here, it's health. Luzardo has Tommy John on his resume, he's missed starts each of the past two seasons with small ailments, and the A's have been loathe to stretch him out. If he stays healthy, look out. He's one of the very few minor leaguers with legitimate No. 1 upside, and a guy Oakland fans will surely cherish—at least until he hits arbitration.

YEAR	TEAM	LVL	AGE	WHIP	ERA	DRA	WARP	MPH	FB%	WHF	CSP
2017	NAT	RK	19	1.02	1.32	3.00	0.4				
2017	ATH	RK	19	0.86	1.54	2.17	0.5				
2017	VER	A-	19	0.89	2.00	2.75	0.5				
2018	STO	A+	20	0.75	1.23	1.88	0.6				
2018	MID	AA	20	0.97	2.29	2.70	2.4				
2018	NAS	AAA	20	2.00	7.31	7.75	-0.4				
2019	STO	A+	21	0.60	0.90	2.19	0.3				
2019	LVG	AAA	21	1.19	3.19	2.57	1.2				
2019	OAK	MLB	21	0.67	1.50	3.32	0.3	98.5	48.5	15.2	45
2020	OAK	MLB	22	1.26	3.73	4.00	2.1	98.5	50.6	15.8	46.9

Oakland Athletics 2020

LINEOUTS

Hitters

HITTER	POS	TEAM	LVL	AGE	PA	R	2B	3B	HR	RBI	BB	K	SB	CS	AVG/OBP/SLG	DRC+	WARP
Luis Barrera	CF	MID	AA	23	240	35	9	11	4	24	12	48	9	7	.321/.357/.513	136	1.1
Skye Bolt	OF	OAK	MLB	25	11	1	1	0	0	0	1	3	0	0	.100/.182/.200	77	0.0
	OF	LVG	AAA	25	347	57	19	3	11	61	37	94	7	5	.269/.350/.459	81	1.1
Seth Brown	1B	OAK	MLB	26	83	11	8	2	0	13	7	23	1	0	.293/.361/.453	83	0.1
	1B	LVG	AAA	26	500	101	29	6	37	104	38	127	8	1	.297/.352/.634	112	1.6
Greg Deichmann	OF	MID	AA	24	340	42	10	2	11	36	34	103	19	5	.219/.300/.375	91	0.7
Dustin Fowler	OF	LVG	AAA	24	606	98	22	7	25	89	42	145	12	4	.277/.333/.477	82	0.5
Ryan Goins	2B	CHA	MLB	31	163	13	6	1	2	10	17	44	0	1	.250/.333/.347	75	0.1
	2B	CHR	AAA	31	316	47	23	2	10	48	39	77	3	3	.322/.406/.531	130	2.9
Jonah Heim	C	MID	AA	24	208	20	12	0	5	34	24	27	0	1	.282/.370/.431	137	2.3
	C	LVG	AAA	24	119	22	9	0	4	19	11	18	0	0	.358/.412/.557	125	1.0
Chris Herrmann	C	LVG	AAA	31	58	14	3	1	4	13	6	18	0	0	.333/.397/.667	113	0.2
	C	OAK	MLB	31	94	9	3	0	1	8	9	29	0	0	.202/.280/.274	64	-0.3
Kyle McCann	C	AGO	Rk	21	25	10	2	2	2	7	5	6	0	0	.400/.520/1.000	169	0.2
	C	VER	A-	21	225	23	7	1	7	25	25	81	0	0	.192/.289/.343	85	0.0
Marcus Smith	OF	AGO	Rk	18	119	21	6	1	0	14	20	29	1	1	.361/.466/.443	164	0.6

Be careful not to scout the stat line with **Luis Barrera**, who always posts solid numbers but doesn't project to have the bat or the power to start full-time. He's fast as heck with a 70 arm though, so he should have a big-league role, possibly as early as 2020. ⚾ **Skye Bolt** recorded his first and heretofore only career hit last May. On that occasion, the bat boy took the unusual step of handing Bolt a letterman's jacket, at which point the exuberant batsman donned the coat, flexed his biceps, raised his arms and exclaimed "SKYE BOLT!" ⚾ **Seth Brown** arrived out of nowhere to run an .815 OPS over nearly 100 plate appearances in the season's final month, strong enough play to deserve an honorable mention in BP's Vogelsong Awards. The guess here is that the power doesn't translate well enough for him to be more of an up-and-down guy over the long haul. ⚾ Nine homers in 23 Fall League games rescued an otherwise disappointing season for **Greg Deichmann**, a positionless power hitter with a, uh, whiff of up-and-down guy to him. ⚾ **Dustin Fowler** was a top-100 prospect at the time of his debut, when he crashed into a wall and tore his patellar tendon. Grim as it is to say, he hasn't looked like the same player since. ⚾ **Ryan Goins** hit his last extra-base hit of the 2019 season on August 24, and ended his year with a 75 DRC+ that propelled him right back into the light-hitting veteran minor-league deal market from whence he emerged. A brief sign of offensive life will keep him within firing range of drawing a major league check in 2020, which was the goal all along. ⓑ **Jonah Heim** had a backup catcher starter kit when he was drafted six years ago. After a good season in the high minors, it appears that Oakland will assemble the final pieces sometime in 2020. ⓑ On Pentecost Island in Vanuatu, there is a custom where men climb a wooden tower, attach their limbs to vines, and leap toward the ground below. Those whose chests scrape the dirt earn the utmost respect for their daring and bravery; rumors that the one furthest from the ground is forced to wear the community's **Chris Herrmann** shirsey for an entire calendar year were unsubstantiated at press time. ⓑ **Kyle McCann** was drafted as a catcher, but he's likely a first basemen, and he'll head to Beloit next spring. For a metaphor on how Oakland's bat-first prospects have coped with that assignment lately, please direct your attention to the burning pile of tires adjacent to Harry C. Pohlman Field. ⓑ Oakland's 2018 third-rounder, **Marcus Smith** was a nifty find out of a Kansas City high school. Scouts weren't sure how he'd fare against professional pitching, but he looked surprisingly advanced in the AZL, showing off a feel for the barrel alongside 70 speed. He's young but promising.

Oakland Athletics 2020

Pitchers

PITCHER	TEAM	LVL	AGE	W	L	SV	G	GS	IP	H	HR	BB/9	K/9	K	GB%	WHIP	ERA	DRA	WARP
Paul Blackburn	LVG	AAA	25	11	3	0	24	22	132^2	133	18	2.3	6.2	92	54%	1.26	4.34	3.24	4.4
	OAK	MLB	25	0	2	0	4	1	11	19	3	3.3	6.5	8	55%	2.09	10.64	5.60	0.0
Marco Estrada	STO	A+	35	0	1	0	3	3	6^2	9	3	1.4	10.8	8	36%	1.50	8.10	6.09	-0.1
	OAK	MLB	35	0	2	0	5	5	23^2	23	7	3.0	4.2	11	20%	1.31	6.85	8.89	-0.8
Grant Holmes	MID	AA	23	6	5	0	22	16	81^2	71	9	3.0	8.4	76	52%	1.20	3.31	4.78	0.1
Brian Howard	MID	AA	24	8	8	0	23	23	130	137	7	2.7	8.2	118	42%	1.35	3.25	5.50	-0.9
	LVG	AAA	24	0	1	0	4	4	14^1	28	4	5.0	10.0	16	36%	2.51	13.81	9.27	-0.4
Jhenderson Hurtado	VER	A-	23	3	0	1	7	0	23^1	12	1	3.9	13.1	34	42%	0.94	0.77	2.79	0.6
	BLT	A	23	1	1	1	7	5	31	22	1	3.8	11.0	38	32%	1.13	2.61	3.61	0.5
Aiden McIntyre	BLT	A	23	3	10	1	27	22	112^2	99	5	6.1	12.0	150	42%	1.55	4.15	5.94	-1.1
Daniel Mengden	LVG	AAA	26	4	3	0	13	10	64	56	8	2.8	8.6	61	53%	1.19	4.22	2.41	2.6
	OAK	MLB	26	5	2	1	13	9	59^2	59	7	4.1	6.3	42	38%	1.44	4.83	7.47	-1.1
Miguel Romero	LVG	AAA	25	4	1	3	45	1	72^2	65	11	4.5	10.0	81	49%	1.39	3.96	3.31	2.1
Jaime Schultz	OKL	AAA	28	2	3	4	47	1	47^2	52	3	5.1	11.7	62	49%	1.66	5.85	2.99	1.5
	LAN	MLB	28	0	0	0	4	0	5	6	1	5.4	5.4	3	25%	1.80	7.20	6.85	-0.1
Chasen Shreve	MEM	AAA	28	2	2	3	51	0	60	45	6	3.9	10.2	68	32%	1.18	3.45	2.54	2.1
	SLN	MLB	28	1	0	0	3	0	2	2	0	4.5	9.0	2	0%	1.50	9.00	5.93	0.0
Gus Varland	STO	A+	22	2	1	0	5	4	26^1	23	3	2.7	9.2	27	37%	1.18	2.39	4.20	0.2
J.B. Wendelken	LVG	AAA	26	6	3	3	30	1	38^2	47	8	4.4	10.0	43	46%	1.71	5.59	5.60	0.2
	OAK	MLB	26	3	1	0	27	0	32^2	21	2	2.5	9.4	34	38%	0.92	3.58	4.12	0.4

Paul Blackburn's 4.34 ERA was the eighth-best mark in the PCL among hurlers who made at least 15 starts, which says all you need to know about both Blackburn and the PCL last season. ⓥ We have a deep field for the "That guy was an All-Star four years ago?" award this spring, but my money is on **Marco Estrada**. ⓥ **Daniel Gossett** posted a 5.91 ERA in 25 starts in 2017-18, and after missing all of last year with an injury, he'll seek to recapture that form in 2020. ⓥ The best thing about **Grant Holmes** is his hair. That could be true even if he was still a big-time prospect, but it's a more damning statement than it used to be. ⓥ **Brian Howard** is probably just a No. 5 starter, but he's a fun one. He's 6-foot-9 and has some natural deception in his delivery. Between that and surprisingly good control for such a lanky dude, he's awkward to face and that helps him survive with fringy stuff. ⓥ **Jhenderson Hurtado** was assigned to and subsequently scratched from the Arizona Fall League. That was disappointing:

After a breakout season, it would have been fun to see how Hurtado's sharp curve and unconventional delivery would have fared against good competition. Ⓐ In Little League, you'll sometimes see a big kid who throws too hard—not just for the batter, but also the catcher, umpire, and strike zone. **Aiden McIntyre** is the A-ball equivalent. Ⓐ Right ho! Saw this young sport called **Daniel Mengden** take the box for his debut against the Red Stockings in '16. Wrote down 'None too impressed,' in the ol' diary that very evening, 'this yannigan will never make good.' Three years on and he's yet to prove that proclamation incorrect. Shame, really; nice fellow with a delightful handlebar." Ⓐ **Miguel Romero** throws a knuckle changeup, a charming detail that separates him from the rest of the right-handed minor league relievers with control problems. Ⓐ **Jaime Schultz** is anonymous enough as a baseball player that you're more likely to call to mind Charles Schulz. Allow us to merge the two: Schultz struggled so badly that he was about one hard-hit ball away from getting undressed by those rockets whizzing around him, not unlike Charlie Brown himself. Ⓐ **Chasen Shreve** is the rare pitcher who causes both dataheads (spin rate) and batters (home-run rate) to drool over him. That combination should make him popular on the waiver wire—and in opposing dugouts. Ⓐ **Gus Varland** entered 2019 as a sleeper, and after making only five appearances in the Cal League, he's now a sleeper with a history of arm trouble. When healthy he hits the mid-90s with two usable breaking balls, and he may be able to start. Ⓐ **J.B. Wendelken** isn't a flight attendant on the route between Oakland and Las Vegas, but he's taken the trip enough to know the job pretty well by now. He's pitched well enough to get a full-time shot in the bullpen, and now out of options, 2020 may be his best chance to do so.

Athletics Prospects

The State of the System
We aren't sure yet, but this is potentially the most average system in baseball.

The Top Ten

★ ★ ★ *2020 Top 101 Prospect* **#9** ★ ★ ★

1 Jesus Luzardo   **LHP**   OFP: 70   ETA: 2019
Born: 09/30/97   Age: 22   Bats: L   Throws: L   Height: 6'0"   Weight: 209
Origin: Round 3, 2016 Draft (#94 overall)

The Report: A southpaw with three potential plus pitches. That's it, man. That's the report.

It's all you need, but we here at the Baseball Prospectus Prospect Team aren't exactly known for restraint when it comes to describing the best prospects in baseball. So with that in mind…

The fastball is easy mid 90s as a starter. There wasn't any more noticeable effort when he was dialing it up to 98-99 out of the major league bullpen late last season. Luzardo can run it into righties, or turn it over with some arm-side wiggle. The command is plus. He keeps the pitch down where it shows some sink. He can elevate it for Ks. The curveball is a power breaker with slider velocity and big lateral break. If you want to nitpick, it doesn't always show ideal depth from his three-quarters slot, but the velocity and command of the pitch should get it to plus regardless. The change comes in even harder, but still has around 10 mph of separation from the fastball and above-average dive. It's the pitch here most in need of refinement, but we are only talking about refinement.

Luzardo is a shorter lefty with a bad injury track record, and looked so good in the pen that you'd be tempted to make him your modern fireman, but he should get every chance to start in 2020, and as long as he has a shot to start, he's one of the best starting pitching prospects in baseball.

Variance: Medium. Luzardo has had arm issues recently. He had a Tommy John surgery right out of high school. He's never thrown more than 109 1/3 innings in a season. There's some risk he might just be one of the better late inning arms in baseball. There's also some risk he gets hurt again and never reaches his enormous potential. On the other hand if he puts it all together, he's one of the few arms I'll throw the "ace upside" tag on.

Mark Barry's Fantasy Take: With all due respect to dudes like MacKenzie Gore or Casey Mize, Luzardo is my favorite dynasty pitching prospect in the game. Sure, I would've preferred if he tossed a few more innings in 2019, and the injuries aren't fun (feels like I'm trying to talk myself out of this, but I promise you, I'm not), but Luzardo should start the season in the rotation, and the domination should shortly follow. Mid-90's heat with two solid secondaries and plus command? Yes, I will sign up for that.

─────── ★ ★ ★ *2020 Top 101 Prospect* **#17** ★ ★ ★ ───────

2 **A.J. Puk   LHP**   OFP: 70   ETA: 2019
Born: 04/25/95   Age: 25   Bats: L   Throws: L   Height: 6'7"   Weight: 238
Origin: Round 1, 2016 Draft (#6 overall)

The Report: Hey it's another lefty with no-shit power stuff. Puk started rehab from his 2018 Tommy John surgery in June, and stormed to the majors by the end of August. His fastball sits a tick higher than even Luzardo's, regularly registering upper 90s on your Stalker. An upper-90s fastball would rarely be described as sneaky fast, as it's just fast-fast, but Puk's length and long stride creates a nightmare angle and release point for batters. 98 gets on you fast regardless, but Puk's gets on you even faster. The long levers have led to control and command issues, and the fastball can run a little true at times, but it's still an easy 70 with elite potential if he corrals the command even a bit more.

Puk's slider is another potential plus-plus weapon in his holster. It routinely touches 90 and tunnels well off the fastball. It's not a big breaker, but the firmness and tilt make it a true swing-and-miss offering. The changeup will flash plus, but doesn't have much fade to it and here the firmness—it also hovers near 90—can sometimes make it seem like just a below-average fastball. At other times there's enough sink and velo separation to make it a real asset. Puk also offers a "slower" curveball in the low 80s for a different breaking ball look. It can get a bit lazy at times, but it's a useful change of pace offering in light of his other three pitches.

Puk's main issue has been the fineness of the command and the control profile, and a guy that size is never going to be Bob Tewksbury. The stuff is good enough he can be a top-of-the-rotation arm with a 10% walk rate, but it's a fine line between effectively wild and inefficiently wild. His late-season cameo could be a preview of what he could look like as a lights out closer, but like with Luzardo, give him every chance to start. And coming off Tommy John, he needs the innings anyway.

Variance: Medium. Puk was functionally still on Tommy John rehab while blowing guys away in the majors in September. On the one hand, the recent elbow issues are a red flag. On the other, he might get more comfortable with the breaking stuff and command when he's another six months out from the surgery date. On the, uh, third hand, he hasn't really answered the question of whether he will throw enough strikes to start yet.

Mark Barry's Fantasy Take: Top-shelf stuff, gaudy strikeout numbers, cringe-inducing WHIP potential, debut stints in the bullpen, uh, long hair—sounds a lot like the Josh Hader recipe for bullpen stud-ness. To be fair, I like Puk quite a bit more than I liked Hader at this point in their respective careers, but the similarities are stark. Anecdotally, the control is the last thing to come back after Tommy John surgery, so maybe Puk will refine some of the mechanical issues that lead to high charitability. If the walks persist, he's probably a reliever. A very, very good reliever, mind you, but a reliever nonetheless.

───── ★ ★ ★ *2020 Top 101 Prospect* **#44** ★ ★ ★ ─────

3 **Sean Murphy C** OFP: 60 ETA: 2019
Born: 10/10/94 Age: 25 Bats: R Throws: R Height: 6'3" Weight: 232
Origin: Round 3, 2016 Draft (#83 overall)

The Report: Murphy dealt with knee issues on and off all year, eventually requiring surgery for a torn meniscus. Once he got back on the field, though, he mashed in Triple-A and won the lion's share of the A's catching job in September. Murphy is one of the best defensive catchers in the minors, and should quickly become one of the better ones in the majors. It's a large frame by backstop standards, but he's athletic and a solid receiver. He gets out of his crouch well and combines it with a well above-average, accurate arm. He also gets high marks for working with pitchers.

The glove alone would make him a viable starting catcher, but Murphy has some juice in his bat as well. He's a big, strong kid who swings hard, and while it isn't the easiest plus raw you'll see, there's 20+ bombs in the stroke due to plus bat speed and loft. The swing does get long and can be a little one-gear, so swing-and-miss is going to be the trade off for the dingers. The plate approach is strong as well, though, and there's the outline of a Three True Outcomes power bat here, which is more than enough to make him a plus regular behind the plate given the rest of the profile. And if Murphy finds a way to hit .270 now and again, he will make some all-star games.

Variance: Medium. Catchers are weird, but Murphy's defense is good enough that he could give you only .240 with 15 home runs and be a perfectly reasonable starter. There's more upside than that in the bat. He's also a 25-year-old catcher already dealing with knee problems.

Mark Barry's Fantasy Take: Murphy wasn't a trainwreck in his first stint behind the dish in Oakland, which is, you know, good (How's that for faint praise?). To be honest, I like Murphy. In a vacuum he has the skills to be a top-10 dude behind the plate, and the defensive skills to get plenty of chances. However, he's hurt more than the dude from the Operation game, and donning the tools of ignorance isn't typically conducive to preserving one's health. I'd have Murphy in the top-five (maybe even the top-three) dynasty catching prospects, but I'll also be holding my breath any time he hits or catches or when someone looks at him the wrong way.

4. Nick Allen SS
OFP: 55 ETA: 2021
Born: 10/08/98 Age: 21 Bats: R Throws: R Height: 5'9" Weight: 166
Origin: Round 3, 2017 Draft (#81 overall)

The Report: After selecting Allen in the third round of the 2017 amateur draft, Oakland convinced the SoCal prep infielder to forego his USC commitment. Long saddled with a reputation as a glove-over-bat shortstop, Allen was just as impressive offensively during an injury-limited campaign in the 2019 Cal League season. The 21-year-old infielder continues to mature physically and add strength to his listed 5-foot-9, 166-pound physique. Often batting at the top of the lineup, Allen's offensive profile works best as a tablesetter; he works counts, gets on base, and scores runs with a little help from his friends. The swing is compact and quick, and quality bat-to-ball supplements his patience to help the hit tool play up. Once aboard, Allen uses quickness and cunning to steal bases and be a general nuisance to opposing pitchers and defenses. A shortstop by nature, he logged a couple dozen games at second base as part of a semi-platoon with Stockton teammate Jeremy Eierman this past season. Allen's foundation of athleticism, adept fielding actions, and capable arm strength provide a path to above-average or better play at the six, and ensure he will thrive at any position in the infield if deployed in a utility role. Ultimately, his advanced baseball instincts and acumen should accelerate his offensive progression and have him ready to contribute at the big league-level by 2021.

Variance: Medium. The sturdy base of 'good defensive middle infielder' limits risk, however stalled offensive progress could result in a replaceable, light-hitting infielder a la Rafael Belliard.

Please don't confuse this guy with the Nick Allen that spent time behind the plate for the Cincinnati Reds in 1920, because rest assured, this is not that Nick Allen. He wasn't all that interesting heading into last season as a glove-first middle infielder, but a strong season with the stick surely perked up my ears. He's not going to hit for much, if any, power, but Allen could be a threat to steal 20 bags with a strong batting average, which means he needs to be on your radar.

5. Austin Beck OF
OFP: 55 ETA: Early 2022
Born: 11/21/98 Age: 21 Bats: R Throws: R Height: 6'1" Weight: 200
Origin: Round 1, 2017 Draft (#6 overall)

The Report: Oakland used the sixth-overall pick of the 2017 Draft to select Beck, a high school outfielder from North Carolina, before other notable first-round picks Keston Hiura and Jo Adell. The 20-year-old outfielder's 2019 Cal League campaign was interrupted by injury on multiple occasions, limiting him to just 85 games with inconsistent production when he was on the field. When healthy, the lean 6-foot-1, 200-pound athlete roams center field, showing plus range, efficient routes, and an above-average throwing arm. He could easily shift to either corner outfield position, but is suited for center thanks to his natural athleticism.

Offensively, Beck employs a gap-to-gap hitting approach and a level swing that limits the game utility of his strength-driven raw power, but does promote hard contact. His swing can still get lengthy, leading to inconsistent rates and quality of contact. The approach remains unrefined and aggressive; his 126 strikeouts and 24 walks in 338 at-bats this past season reflect his free-swinging mentality and inconsistent bat-to-ball skills. After contact, Beck's 60-grade speed allows him to hustle into plenty of extra bases, although he's yet to refine his base-stealing abilities. With advanced outfield defense and baserunning, it will be Beck's offensive progression that will dictate his big league ETA. The upside here is a plus-defending outfielder with a run-producing bat, though the latter half of that equation will take some time to flesh out even in a best-case scenario. At his current rate, the athletic center fielder should be ready to contribute at the big league level by late-2021 or the spring of 2022.

Variance: High. The hit tool is always difficult to handicap due to its blatant unpredictability. Beck's foundation of raw athleticism provides a certain degree of comfort, but his baseball-specific skills need further nurturing and cultivation.

Mark Barry's Fantasy Take: A defense-first athlete that just needs to learn how to hit. Where do I sign up? Kidding.

Beck struck out over 34 percent of the time at High-A last season, which leaves me bearish on his ability to hit enough to put his athleticism to work, especially in a fantasy sense. I don't typically have a penchant for giving up on 20-year-old, top-10 picks, but I'm kinda close on Beck.

Jorge Mateo SS OFP: 55   ETA: 2020
Born: 06/23/95   Age: 25   Bats: R   Throws: R   Height: 6'0"   Weight: 192
Origin: International Free Agent, 2012

The Report: I have been writing about Jorge Mateo so long that I'm half-sure I made a shoebox diorama of him stealing second base in the Tampa complex for a sixth grade class project. You might look at the 19 home runs this year—more than his 2017 and 2018 combined—and give credit to the new Triple-A ball and move from Nashville to Las Vegas for his 2019 home games. That probably explains some of the power bump, but Mateo has gotten stronger and added loft to his swing, so fringe or maybe even average game power isn't out of the realm of possibility now. How much the newfound pop plays in the majors remains an open question as his overaggressive approach is still here and may get exploited by the best arms in the world. The Yankees experimented with Mateo in the outfield, but the A's have essentially made him their Triple-A starting shortstop, with the occasional reps at second mixed in. He remains a passable if rough

Oakland Athletics 2020

fit there, but he's not displacing Marcus Semien anyway. His speed remains a true weapon, although he's not the volume base-stealer he was in the low minors—possibly because he's not on base as much. Overall, it was a bounce back year for Mateo and he's basically ready for a superutility or fifth infield role on a good team.

Variance: Medium. That's high for a guy with two seasons of Triple-A under his belt but there are still unanswered questions about the hit tool utility against better stuff. The other part of the variance here is Mateo is the type of profile that might be significantly impacted by which baseballs Rawlings decides to put on the assembly line next year. Projecting that is out of my purview.

Mark Barry's Fantasy Take: It would be awesome if you could take, like, five percentage points from Mateo's strikeout rate and tack them on to his walk rate, but alas, we don't have the technology for that yet. The increase of power this season is encouraging, but his fantasy relevance is, and always will be, tied to his ability to get on base to utilize his blazing speed. Let's welcome Mateo back to the top-150ish and cross our fingers that he can get on base more than 30 percent of the time.

7 Robert Puason SS   OFP: 60   ETA: 2024ish
Born: 09/11/02   Age: 17   Bats: B   Throws: R   Height: 6'3"   Weight: 165
Origin: International Free Agent, 2019

The Report: I first wrote about Robert Puason back in 2017, almost two years before he was eligible to sign with a major-league organization. By that time, his agent had already agreed to an illegal deal with the Atlanta Braves that involved international cap circumvention. The Braves were subsequently barred from signing him, and general manager John Coppolella was banned for life as part of the greater scandal. According to ESPN's Jeff Passan, Robert Puason was just 13 when that deal was struck.

A short time after Atlanta was barred from signing Puason, word started spreading throughout the industry that he had a deal for similar money with Oakland. As it almost always does with high profile July 2 signings, the word turned out to be correct, and the A's spent the vast majority of their pool on him earlier this year.

In the intervening time since Puason became a prominent prospect and agreed to these deals and when they were actually signed, Jasson Dominguez has passed him as a prospect. He's still generally considered the second-best player from the 2019-20 J2 talent pool, a projectable and toolsy infielder. Like with Dominguez, we just really don't have a whole lot to go on here because he hasn't seen real game action quite yet, although he did play in instructs. We do think he probably deserves to be ranked somewhere, and this is our best guess as to where that is.

But we simply cannot ignore the elephant in the room here, either. It is inherently wrong to be locking 13-year-olds up in handshake agreements years in advance of when you can actually sign them, with no protections and the burden entirely on the player. It's just wrong, and MLB has chosen to turn the other way on this and only care about pool manipulation instead. And that is a big part of Puason's story.

Variance: Extreme. There's nothing here that's all that different from Kevin Maitan at the same age—right down to the illegal early deal with Atlanta—and you probably know how that turned out.

Mark Barry's Fantasy Take: Like many J2 teenagers, lots of Puason's skills have been shrouded in secrecy, or at least grainy YouTube clips and vague "I Love How He Plays" statements from the team. Also like J2 teenagers, his value is bound to be artificially goosed. I'd have him in the first 8-10 picks for first year player drafts this winter, but not in the top five.

8   Daulton Jefferies   RHP   OFP: 55   ETA: Late 2020

Born: 08/02/95   Age: 24   Bats: L   Throws: R   Height: 6'0"   Weight: 182
Origin: Round 1, 2016 Draft (#37 overall)

The Report: Jefferies finally got back on the mound after a 2017 Tommy John surgery followed by rehab issues in 2018. Durability questions were present even before the Tommy John, as he's a shorter, leaner righty who had shoulder issues in college. The volume has only been turned up there after missing almost two full seasons, but the good news is the stuff has come back. The fastball sits mid 90s in short bursts. It can run a little true, but occasionally flashes a bit of arm-side hop. The command profile isn't great either due to his short arm action and crossfire delivery.

Jeffries best secondary is a hard cutter that will flash slider-like two-plane action. He also mixes in a 11-6 curve around 80, which can be a bit of an up-and-under, humpy offering, but shows decent depth and gives a different breaking ball look and a different velo band for hitters to deal with. He rounds out the four-pitch mix with a firm changeup which lacks ideal velocity separation—it routinely hits 90—but offers wiffle-ball-like hard fade and dive when he turns it over.

Jeffries has a squint-and-you-can-see-it arsenal of four average-or-better pitches, but the likelihood is they don't all actually get there, and the injury track record might mean he's better suited to shorter outings. For now he needs more healthy innings, period. We'll check back after 2020, but 2019 was a success, albeit qualified.

Variance: Very high. His last healthy season was 2015, his sophomore year at Cal. There are reliever markers in the delivery and frame, and the fastball can run a little true and play down from the plus velo it shows. But if he's actually healthy and puts it together in 2020, the stuff isn't all that dissimilar from your backend 101 type.

Oakland Athletics 2020

Mark Barry's Fantasy Take: Jeffries flashes some decent skills and has certainly posted impressive strikeout numbers. But the whole "Only Pitched 20 1/3 innings from 2016-2018" thing makes him a risk I'm not taking. His proximity could keep him in the Top-200 range, but he's not there for me.

9   Sheldon Neuse   3B   OFP: 50   ETA: 2019
Born: 12/10/94   Age: 25   Bats: R   Throws: R   Height: 6'0"   Weight: 218
Origin: Round 2, 2016 Draft (#58 overall)

The Report: The A's acquired Neuse in 2017 and aggressively assigned him to Triple-A the following season after he'd logged just a dozen and a half games in the Texas League, and it didn't work out so well at the time. The former second-rounder promptly got exposed by better velocity and guile, and offensive struggles snowballed for the better part of the year before a late surge in the second half. And lo, the moon ball cameth; Neuse was able to get his approach development back on track last season while tapping into zero-gravity power. It's a relatively compact swing with a minimal load and quick hips that produce some bat speed, and while he still puts the ball on the ground too much he's learned to better leverage himself in hitting counts, so there's cause for hope that last year's over-the-fence outburst wasn't entirely context-driven. He's a solid if unspectacular third baseman, and the club started to move him around a bit last season with reps at second, short (where he played in college), and even a couple glimpses in left. The versatility can only help his quest to carve out a regular role, and the best-case scenario has him contributing average defensive value across a couple spots, hitting some bombs, and playing a solid, everyday role. In the meantime, he can plug in for the A's whenever they need him next season and try again to slow down big-league pitching and get his career rolling in The Show.

Variance: Medium. It's not that there's a huge amount of volatility here, it's just not the most unique of profiles or dynamic of skill sets for the role. He's ready to roll, but the downside is an up-and-down guy.

Mark Barry's Fantasy Take: Lazy teammate comp time! I get some Chad Pinder vibes from Neuse (with maybe slightly higher upside). If that leaves you cold, that's ok, I'm a little chilly too. The potential positional flexibility makes Neuse an AL-only stash, but I'm not running out to grab him elsewhere.

10   Logan Davidson   SS   OFP: 50   ETA: 2022
Born: 12/26/97   Age: 22   Bats: B   Throws: R   Height: 6'3"   Weight: 185
Origin: Round 1, 2019 Draft (#29 overall)

The Report: The draft day consensus pegged Davidson as a tall, switch-hitting shortstop with some athleticism and pop but a questionable hit tool. The current consensus is he's a tall, switch-hitting shortstop with some athleticism and pop but a questionable hit tool. He struggled badly in the Penn League outside of a torrid week and a half stretch, and at the time some scouts were hypothesizing his long season and small Vermont crowds might be the culprit. I'm personally a bit skeptical of that reasoning, as Davidson's issues are more related to his timing and long swing. He utilizes a quiet load which likely isn't ideal for his long-limbed body, as the body can get stiff as the pitcher begins his throwing motion. His underwhelming professional debut only serves as a continuation of poor wood bat performance spanning back to his Cape Cod days.

All this said, we'd be doing a disservice by not highlighting the attractive characteristics in the profile, characteristics which are first round-worthy: there is above-average raw power from both sides of the plate, and he plays an adequate defensive shortstop. He drove the ball to all fields in the ACC, and doing so in pro ball will be key as he moves up the ladder.

Variance: High. There are real concerns about the hit tool that could require a swing adjustment. That's easier said than done for switch-hitters.

Mark Barry's Fantasy Take: After questions about his hit tool, Davidson posted a .239 batting average in his first 238 trips to the plate. He did walk a lot though, and the potential power/speed combo is fun to dream on. That said, it's a little like buying the body of a race car with a Ford Escort engine (might be harsh, but whatever). A league needs 250+ prospects for me to take a flier on Davidson.

The Next Five

11
Lazaro Armenteros OF
Born: 05/22/99   Age: 21   Bats: R   Throws: R   Height: 6'0"   Weight: 182
Origin: International Free Agent, 2016

On one hand, Armenteros drips strength and physicality; at 20 he's already filled out plenty, and it's just one of those bodies that was built to grow more and more muscle through his 20s. He's got some quicker-twitch aesthetics to his movements now, though he's likely to stiffen some as he matures into the gobs of top-half strength left to come, and his presently above-average straight line speed should fade a bit. His age also earns him some slack for the year's performance, as he was one of the younger regulars in his High-A league. Caveats notwithstanding, though, it was a really rough year to watch. The swing mechanics are often disjointed, with a high back shoulder that can create awkward angles into the zone when he's slightly off-time, and a tight bottom hand that'll get too strong and leave the barrel dragging under balls on the regular. There are significant swaths of the zone in which he's currently vulnerable, and he also showed plenty of willingness to expand above and below it without much improvement as the season wore on. Despite his strength the throw tool isn't great, so it's a left field profile, and he wasn't especially consistent at reading contact or judging trajectory in that corner this year. All of this is to say that he's still really, really raw. The physicality is such that it could

Oakland Athletics 2020

very well click and turn into an impressive package. But that's unlikely to happen quickly, and his will be one of the more interesting developmental journeys in the system next year.

12 Grant Holmes   RHP
Born: 03/22/96   Age: 24   Bats: L   Throws: R   Height: 6'0"   Weight: 224
Origin: Round 1, 2014 Draft (#22 overall)

Holmes at 12 in this system represents the prospect version of a waystation. Injuries have plagued the righty, but 2019 also included more flashes of his first-round talent. His recovery from rotator cuff surgery included spending most of his time in Double-A Midland, where he came out innings-limited and gradually worked his way up to more robust outings before finishing up with a single Triple-A Las Vegas start. The velocity and pitch quality at season's open looked wonky, but as time went on and the surgery fell further into the rearview Holmes began to find it a little more regularly. When it's working it's the same moving fastball/okay cutter/downer curve combo that propelled his early career, but he made impressive strides in keeping that arsenal in the zone—an issue that has long limited his when-healthy development. Injuries will be a valid risk factor to consider at every step on his path, but the sum total of this age-23 season was a large and encouraging one in the right direction. Next season will be about maintaining his consistency gains, staying on the bump long enough to improve on them, and potentially seeing how it plays against major leaguers. It's hard to imagine Holmes doesn't start his 2020 campaign in Las Vegas, and with Oakland's seemingly fearless nature about advancement, Holmes could see the big leagues sooner than later. It's also been long enough into this writeup to tell you that Holmes has amazing hair, if you didn't already know. The #flow is an easy 7, and the best of Holmes' tools without question. If he can ride the waves on his scalp, he's never gonna fail.

13 Alfonso Rivas   1B/OF
Born: 09/13/96   Age: 23   Bats: L   Throws: L   Height: 6'0"   Weight: 188
Origin: Round 4, 2018 Draft (#113 overall)

The A's fourth-round selection in the 2018 Draft out of the University of Arizona, Rivas' polished skill set and high baseball IQ establish a high floor for the first baseman/outfielder. Rivas slashed .292/.387/.423 across two-levels in the 2019 season, including eight late-season games with the Triple-A Las Vegas Aviators where he went 13-for-32 (.406 AVG). The fast-twitch athleticism and manual dexterity that make him a plus-defending first baseman also allowed him to play 11 games in left field this season, adding defensive versatility to his resume. Offensively, Rivas has plus bat-to-ball abilities and a line-to-line approach that enabled him to accumulate 39 extra-base hits, nine of which were long balls. Equipped with his newfound defensive versatility and advanced offensive acumen, Rivas should continue to rapidly matriculate through the Oakland farm system. Considering Matt Olson's current Gold Glove-occupation of first base, Rivas' versatility is vital within the A's organization. Capable of providing quality left-handed at-bats and playing multiple positions, he'd be a valuable contributor off the bench or in a potential trade.

14 James Kaprielian   RHP
Born: 03/02/94   Age: 26   Bats: R   Throws: R   Height: 6'3"   Weight: 210
Origin: Round 1, 2015 Draft (#16 overall)

Kaprielian's stock has had a steady slide over the last few years. Once upon a time, he was flashing top-of-the-rotation stuff, and so much so that he made the 2017 101 despite difficulty staying on the mound. He had Tommy John surgery that spring and was included in the Sonny Gray trade later that year while rehabbing. He proceeded to miss not only all of 2017, but all of 2018 with rehab complications and shoulder troubles. When he finally got back into games this past May, he was still somewhat limited; he only pitched five innings twice all season, and capped out at 73 pitches. He's now more low 90s with occasional bursts into the mid 90s instead of mid-90s-flashing-higher, and the slider is now ahead of the other offspeeds. He's also entering his age-26 season with less than 100 official pro innings after spending the majority of his age-25 campaign pitching truncated outings in High-A. There's still, somehow, an obvious mid-rotation talent level here if he ever can pitch 150 healthy innings in a season, and there's also late-innings potential if he takes to short relief as a fastball/slider type.

15 Luis Barrera   CF
Born: 11/15/95   Age: 24   Bats: L   Throws: L   Height: 6'0"   Weight: 205
Origin: International Free Agent, 2012

The A's threw a big pile of money at Barrera out of the Dominican way back in 2012, and he has travelled through just about every nook and cranny of Oakland's minor league landscape in the years since. Most recently, he's hit .324 in 90 games at Double-A over the past two seasons. He throws arms at pitches, with a handsy left-handed swing that doesn't typically feature a whole lot of plane to it. He clips 200 pounds as a 6-footer, and at 24 he's now filled out considerably over the years. It's conceivable there's some latent power here, though the swing definition isn't really conducive for it at all at present, and he'll be on the comeback from a season-ending shoulder injury when next we see him. He struggled to steal bases last year against advanced batteries, but the speed has held at least plus as he's matured physically, and he tracks balls well in center. He's on the 40-man roster now, and should see a chance to break in during the 2020 season.

Oakland Athletics 2020

16 Tyler Baum RHP
Born: 01/14/98 Age: 22 Bats: R Throws: R Height: 6'2" Weight: 195
Origin: Round 2, 2019 Draft (#66 overall)

Your typical second-round college arm generally falls into one of two categories: i) Good stuff, but not as much polish as you'd expect; and ii) good polish and performance, but not as much stuff as you'd hope. Baum doesn't quite fit in either basket. He was a three year-starter in the ACC, but never really dominated and the stuff is more of the 50-55 variety. You'd expect that arm to have more success in college than he did, and maybe there is some untapped potential with pro instruction, although North Carolina has a reputation as one of the more analytically-minded college programs out there. There's feel for four pitches here and the fastball can touch 95, but the delivery is uptempo with some late effort, so relief risk looms.

17 Skye Bolt OF
Born: 01/15/94 Age: 26 Bats: B Throws: R Height: 6'2" Weight: 187
Origin: Round 4, 2015 Draft (#128 overall)

It's been tough to know quite what to do with Bolt for a long time now, as his is the quintessential case of the early-blooming toolsy kid who never quite actualizes any of those tools in any kind of linear progression. He's battled general inconsistency for much of his professional career, though there have been a bunch of flashes of interesting game talent along the way, including both a huge finishing run to his 2018 season and a monstrous open to this past year, with the latter forcing a big-league debut. There have been and remain across-the-board tools here, and also a lot of caveats. He's a switch-hitter, but the splits are heavily weighted in favor of a left-handed swing that provides a solid rate of line-drive contact and occasional pull-side carry. He's fast, but he hasn't quite developed consistency as a base-stealer or center field route-runner. There's arm strength for right, but even a best-case scenario for the bat's outcome may leave him a little light for the position. The safe bet on the outcome remains that of a fourth- or fifth-outfielder, with second-division upside for stretches if and when the bat's clicking.

18 Greg Deichmann OF
Born: 05/31/95 Age: 25 Bats: L Throws: R Height: 6'2" Weight: 190
Origin: Round 2, 2017 Draft (#43 overall)

IThe A's made a tough decision to keep their former second-rounder on an age-appropriate development curve in Double-A last season after an injury-curtailed and unproductive 2018 season at Stockton, and things didn't go so hot. He continues to show a decent awareness of the strike zone, and the swing is mechanically pretty simple. But there's also some stiffness to it, and he struggled to extend on fastballs and do much damage for most of the year. The arm's fine for right, and he gets moving reasonably well, to where he should be able to hold his own defensively. He's unlikely to add much positive value with the leather, however, so he's really going to need to tap into just about all of his 5:00 o'clock power to make the profile work. He showed flashes of what that looks like against the tired arms of the AFL, but he'll be 25 next year and it'll become increasingly incumbent on him to show it in-season.

19 Jonah Heim   C
Born: 06/27/95   Age: 25   Bats: B   Throws: R   Height: 6'4"   Weight: 220
Origin: Round 4, 2013 Draft (#129 overall)

Originally drafted by the Baltimore Orioles in the fourth round of the 2013 Draft, the switch-hitting catcher is now with his third organization and was recently added to the Athletics' 40-man roster. A plus defender behind the plate, Heim apprehended 52-percent (26-of-50) of attempted base-burglars in 2019 with the help of a rocket throwing arm, often deployed from his knees. After a disastrous Double-A debut with the bat in 2018, the switch-hitting Heim rebounded to hit well at the level before pounding the Triple-A moon ball all around the Mojave Desert. He displays a catcher's approach at the dish and advanced baseball instincts all over the place, and is the most polished out of a nice batch of solid backup catching prospects scattered throughout this system.

20 Jeremy Eierman   SS
Born: 09/10/96   Age: 23   Bats: R   Throws: R   Height: 6'0"   Weight: 205
Origin: Round 2, 2018 Draft (#70 overall)

Oakland Athletics 2020

Oakland's second-round pick out of Missouri State in 2018, Eierman displayed a unique power and speed combination for a shortstop in college, but it has yet to translate to his professional career. It's a durable, athletic frame at 6-feet and 205 pounds, and he swung between both middle-infield positions over the course of the year. He displayed quality lateral quickness and above-average range on both sides of second base, while a big-time arm produces throws with excellent carry through the bag. He shows an advanced internal clock that allows him to slow the game down, and his footwork around the bag is another defensive strength.

Offensively, Eierman has plus raw power and consistently displays it in batting practice. He generates good loft, and can spray the ball gap-to-gap. Far too often he sells out to try and find it in game, however, and there is stiffness and length into the zone off a very deep hand load and little early momentum to the swing. It all works to compromise his timing, and he struggled consistently to catch up to velocity all year. Swing adjustments and some corresponding growth in the offensive projection can bump him up this list a good bit next year, but the hit tool concerns cloud the profile for now.

Personal Cheeseball

PC
Alexander Pantuso   RHP
Born: 10/14/95   Age: 24   Bats: L   Throws: R   Height: 6'6"   Weight: 235
Origin: Round 31, 2018 Draft (#923 overall)

Pantuso is a 24-year-old former 31st-rounder who just logged his first four innings of short-season ball at the end of the season. Are you not entertained? Well, you will be if he can find any semblance of command, because the stuff is almost as huge as his frame now. He leverages every inch of his 6-foot-6, long-levered body with a way, way, over-the-top release point that creates obscene plane and a very difficult angle for barrels to find. His gas now checks in high 90s, while the slider's shape is both weird from the slot and late in showing. Pitch-to-pitch repetition is as spotty as you may imagine coming from that kind of length, but the club will have every incentive to push him quickly, and it'll be neat if it works.

Low Minors Sleeper

LMS
Marcus Smith   OF
Born: 09/11/00   Age: 19   Bats: L   Throws: L   Height: 5'11"   Weight: 190
Origin: Round 3, 2019 Draft (#104 overall)

It's cheating a little bit to throw a club's third-rounder into this slot, but the Kansas City prep pick debuted for all of 29 games in the AZL after signing, and he's a fun player, so he counts. He's the kind of 5-foot-11 that has really strong legs and builds muscle mass well, and he's a 70-grade runner who gets off the blocks and up to speed efficiently in center. It's raw out there, in both his reads and his efforts to harness solid arm strength, but the speed will give him ample opportunity to grow into the leather, and there's potential to eventually add a good chunk of value there. His swing is armsy and quick, with very little lower-half engagement or ability to impact the ball, but he showed ability to take pitches and stay in the zone pretty well while finding the barrel consistently in his debut. Whether he can translate physical strength into any semblance of game thump will be the $400,000 question, and it'll take some evolution to the swing to get there.

Top Talents 25 and Under (as of 4/1/2020)

1. Jesus Luzardo
2. Ramon Laureano
3. Matt Olson
4. A.J. Puk
5. Sean Murphy
6. Franklin Barreto
7. Dustin Fowler
8. Nick Allen
9. Austin Beck
10. Jorge Mateo

This year's 25U looks very similar to last year's. There is still a good amount of young, controllable talent in the system which should make an impact with the big-league club in 2020.

With Matt Chapman graduating and his health returning, Jesús Luzardo claims the top spot in this iteration. Nipping at his heels, though, Ramon Laureano followed up his breakout 2018 debut with a similarly outstanding 2019 campaign. Although Laureano missed about six weeks with a stress fracture in his right shin, he was still highly productive in all phases when healthy, running up 4.2 WARP to rank fourth among all AL center fielders. Laureano's true claim to fame comes from his arm and his ability to throw runners out, but after a tough start to the year he also continued rounding into a solid offensive player with the ability to drive the ball, get on base, and add runs on the basepaths.

Matt Olson has been a mainstay on this list and returns for the 2020 season, making the cut by a matter of days. He also missed 34 games after injuring his hand in the second A's-Mariners game in Japan in March, but when he returned in May he looked productive as ever and appeared to have no lingering effects from the injury. Olson posted a 134 DRC+ over 127 games while winning a Gold Glove at first, confirming that the A's have the corners of their infield taken care of for the foreseeable future.

Oakland Athletics 2020

It feels like Franklin Barreto has been around (and failing against big-league pitching) forever, but he's still only 23 and has logged all of 208 career plate appearances over the past three seasons. Barreto spent the majority of 2019 at Triple-A Las Vegas where he amassed an above-average 108 DRC+ which includes a heavy penalty for the environment, before finally getting another call up in September. He's firmly in the Daulton Pompey zone as a post-prospect guy, but there's still upside as a starting middle infielder and he should get a crack at the Opening Day roster in 2020.

Dustin Fowler can spin a similar yarn after spending all of 2019 in Triple-A a year removed from playing in 69 nice games for the A's the season prior. The A's acquired Fowler in 2017 from the Yankees, the same year in which he ruptured his patellar tendon. It looks more like a tweener profile at this point, and both his offensive and defensive performance stagnated in the desert last season. There's still big league-caliber (and -ready) value to be found here, though.

Part 3: Featured Articles

The Baseball Is Juiced (Again)

Robert Arthur

This article originally appeared at Baseball Prospectus on April 5, 2019.

It started when the normally reliable Chris Sale got lit up for three homers by the Mariners in the Red Sox's season opener. It was part of a record number of taters that flew on Opening Day, as starters from Sale to Zack Greinke were taken deep by the handful. Then Christian Yelich hit a home run in each of his first four games, tying yet another MLB record, this one for consecutive games with a dinger to start a season.

It didn't take long for fans and players to begin whispering and tweeting about the baseballs being juiced again. It's early yet for us to come to any definitive conclusion about the 2019 season, but preliminary data shows that the baseball has returned to its aerodynamic peak. Whether that means this season will smash home run records like 2017 did remains to be seen.

Before home run explosion over the last few years, no one worried too much about the baseball's air resistance. While MLB and Rawlings (the company that manufactures the official baseballs) kept track of dozens of metrics to make sure that the ball was consistent from month to month, they didn't measure drag.

But drag is incredibly important in determining how likely a hitter is to knock one out of the park. As baseballs become more aerodynamic, they travel further given a certain initial velocity. A deep fly ball that might have been caught at the warning track can instead go into the first row of the stands. A three percent change in drag coefficient can work to add about five feet to a well-hit fly ball, which can in turn increase home runs league wide by an astounding 10-15 percent.

It's possible to measure the aerodynamics of the baseball using the pitch-tracking radars currently in place in each MLB ballpark. By calculating the loss of speed from when the pitch is released to when it crosses the plate, you can directly measure the drag coefficient on the baseball. I first wrote about the role of decreasing drag in boosting home runs in 2017, and MLB's commission of scientists and statisticians later confirmed that the more aerodynamic baseballs

Oakland Athletics 2020

in use that year were largely to blame for the spike in home runs. The same commission rejected some alternate hypotheses, like rising temperatures and a league-wide boost in launch angle pushing more balls over the fence.

The current era has featured some large fluctuations in drag coefficient, leading to first an explosion in 2016 and 2017, and then a dialing back of homers last year. Curious about the record-breaking home run tallies in the last few days, I used the same methodology to measure the aerodynamics of the baseballs so far in 2019.

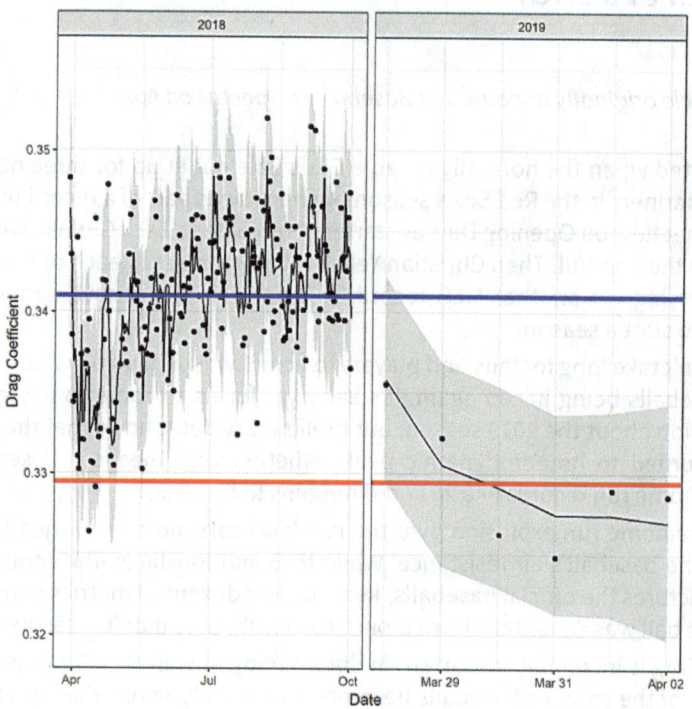

We're only a week into the 2019 season, but the drag numbers so far are among the lowest recorded in the last calendar year. With apologies for gory math, the current 2019 season average drag coefficient (the red line) would be below the 95 percent credible interval (the shaded area) for about nine-tenths of the 2018 season. (I used a Bayesian Random Walk model implemented in INLA to calculate these credible intervals, averaging the drag numbers in each game and adjusting for park.)

There were only a handful of six-day stretches in 2018 that had drag numbers below what we're seeing now, and most were in late June and early July. All of this means that 2019's data so far is quite a bit different than what we saw through most of last year.

These drag coefficients factor out the effects of temperature and air density, so they aren't a product of April cold. However, the numbers could be deceptive if the radars used to track pitches have changed from year to year. I consulted with some experts within baseball who were not aware of any specific modifications to the radar this year that could produce this pattern, but it's an important caveat of which to be aware.

On the one hand, it's only been six days, and we don't quite have the statistical basis to say that these drag coefficients are unprecedented compared to 2018. On the other hand, we've witnessed about 5,000 fastballs so far this season, so it's not as if our sample size is small. At least so far, the baseball has played like it's much more aerodynamic than it was last year. In fact, the current drag coefficient is really only comparable to 2017, when the baseballs were more aerodynamic than they had been in at least a decade.

It's not just fancy radar tracking indicating that the baseball is flying through the air more easily. The current number of home runs per game (as of this writing) is the highest it's been since the heady days of 2017, the year that teams and players broke dinger-related records everywhere you looked. That's especially remarkable considering that we're in what is typically the coldest part of the regular season, when lower temperatures and higher winds tend to suppress offense and keep balls in the air within the park. Comparing only from April to April, this year's rate of home runs per fly ball is even a little bit higher than it was in 2017.

With that said, the current measurements are no guarantee that 2019 will be another year of record-shattering homer hitting. The trouble with the drag measurements is that they are not consistent from June to August, from week to week, or even sometimes from day to day. Whether because of natural manufacturing variation or differences in the underlying supplies of cowhide and thread that go into the baseballs, drag has a tendency to fluctuate up and down over the course of a year. So the homers that fly in the first week of April wouldn't necessarily clear the fence a week later.

It's possible that this one-week drop in drag coefficient subsides and the baseball returns to its 2018 levels. On the other hand, it's almost equally probable that the ball becomes even more slippery and flies ever farther. Either way, it's clear that the baseball's air resistance is something to keep an eye on for the remainder of the 2019 season.

—Robert Arthur is an author of Baseball Prospectus.

The Moral Hazard of Playing It Safe

Craig Goldstein

This article originally appeared at Baseball Prospectus on August 6, 2019.

A couple days prior to the trade deadline, amidst a sea of tranquility posing as the lead up to the trade deadline, Bob Nightengale took to Twitter. Nightengale, who was probably wearing his pants backwards at the time, tweeted that MLB GMs were coming around on the idea that the unified trade deadline should be moved back from July 31 to August 15, so they could better assess their positions in the standings and whether they should buy or sell. To which I said:

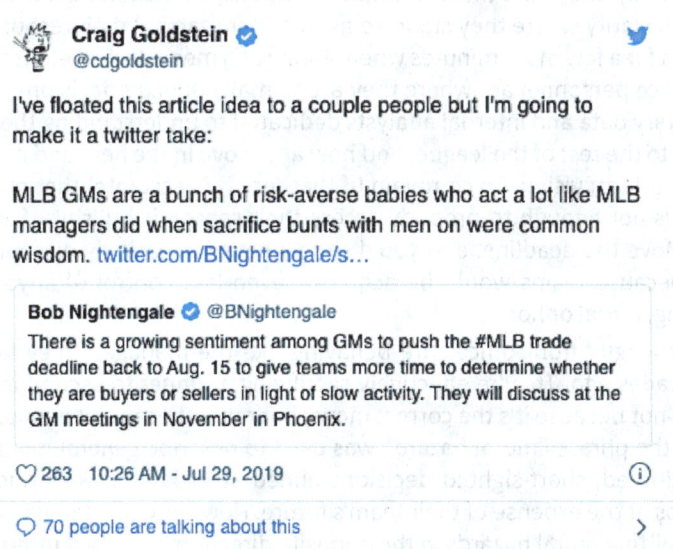

This might strike some as reductive and churlish. And it might be that, but it isn't really wrong, either. Jeff Quinton wrote a great piece discussing the environmental factors that enable front offices to avoid risk without upsetting the apple cart within their own fanbases. I don't believe that it goes far enough, however. His article gives us the proper framework through which to understand why these behaviors have been allowed to seep into front offices throughout the league. Understanding the reasons behind these actions are different from excusing them, though, and GMs should not be let off the hook for their non-competitive approach to the trade deadline (much less the offseason).

⚾   ⚾   ⚾

It's fair to say that fans as a group have rarely, if ever, been pro-player. It is also fair to say that in the time during and following the Moneyball revolution, the pendulum swung from fans who cared intensely about winning in the moment (and thus might be intolerant of a rebuilding approach) to fans who supported building a team that could compete throughout multiple seasons, viewing the playoffs as a crapshoot, with the thought that getting multiple bites at the apple was a better approach than taking a bigger bite in any one season.

There's nothing wrong with that approach, and I still find merit in that argument. However, it seems that the pendulum has swung too far in that direction. Teams are overvaluing some of the individual factors that make themselves long-term contenders rather than attempting to seize a championship when given the opportunity. It's a difficult needle to thread.

And surely, they (and those in similar positions) would have liked another two weeks to clarify where they stand so as to better marshal their resources. We've all asked for a few more minutes when staring at a menu. But all of these GMs and front office personnel are where they are to make difficult decisions. They have proprietary data and internal analysts dedicated to understanding their position relative to the rest of the league, and how any move in the here and now impacts their long-term vision. To complain (if that report is accurate) that over half the season is not enough to properly assess their season is bullshit of the highest order. Move the deadline, and you'd simply have increasingly discounted trade offers because teams would be acquiring even less control of anyone they're acquiring, rental or not.

Major league front offices are behaving like the managers they lampooned two decades ago. They're effectively sacrificing a runner to second in the ninth inning—not because it's the correct move, but rather because it is safe. It used to be that the phrase "moral hazard" was used to describe general managers who made ill-fated, short-sighted decisions aimed at locking in wins and securing their jobs at the expense of their team's future. Now, general managers are guilty of committing moral hazards in the opposite direction, playing it utterly safe and terrified of becoming scapegoats.

In lieu of bold action, they opt to pussyfoot around a current window of contention, choosing instead to play the long game and stack up years of control like they're blocks in a game of Jenga. GMs pass on signing quality players in free agency because the back-end of the deal might look bad, and because they might be able to squeeze out 70 percent of the production from a player who costs a tenth as much. That's a safer investment, too, because it's also hard to prove a negative—it's impossible to prove that Manny Machado would make the Mets a playoff team in 2019-2020, but it's easy to say that the back half of Robinson Cano's contract sucks. Owners, who rule over GM's jobs, are also humans with human brain processes that will always make the so-called albatross contract uglier than the road not taken.

These days, GMs are remembered for the bad deals they make and the surplus value they generate, not the acquisition of expensive, necessary talents that meet their market worth (or fall slightly short while still providing significant on-field value). And front offices know that one or two expensive misfires can cost them their jobs, no matter how many good deals they make.

No front office exemplifies this ethos more than the Toronto Blue Jays. General Manager Ross Atkins had this to say following the Blue Jays underwhelming trade deadline:

This is by no means the first time that an executive will cite years of control to justify their actions, which is often just another way of saying "don't look at what we got, look at how much we got of it." Atkins touts quantity to elide the discussion of quality—either, that of the players acquired, or those given up. Remember: the other teams presumably value years of control, too.

Atkins also had some thoughts to offer regarding free agents back in early 2018:

Oakland Athletics 2020

This ignores, of course, whether the player can create enough value in the front end of a contract to justify the longer term of a deal, and the decline that often occurs in the back end. It also ignores whether the player can fill a need the team requires and put them in a position to compete for and win a championship. But as teams seemingly avoid contention at all, where they might end up having to consider and later justify some of these tough decisions, we still see risk-averse approaches.

Anthony Fenech's article on two trades that recently extended GM Al Avila didn't make got at this issue rather well:

> Passing on those deals was defensible: Both players had yet to break out and trading [Michael] Fulmer—a pitcher who appeared to be a future ace, no matter his injury concerns—would have taken serious gumption, opening Avila up to strong criticism.

Avoiding strong criticism is something each of us can understand as a motivation, but the avoidance of criticism only matters if that criticism is valid. In Fulmer's case, shoving his injury concerns aside affects not only the years that the team controls him (he is currently missing a full season due to Tommy John surgery) but also the quality of those seasons, as his knee and elbow injuries combined to dampen his effectiveness even when healthy enough to pitch. But it was easy to present the then-current image of Fulmer as a top of the rotation pitcher who the team had under its domain for the next five seasons as something to build around. The status quo isn't nearly as often second-guessed as a decision that disrupts it.

⚾   ⚾   ⚾

MLB GMs are risk-averse to a fault. They are ivy-educated and consulting firm-approved, and yet they can't seem to avoid leaving wins on the table in their all-consuming lust for a non-existent $/WAR championship. They are supposed to zig when everyone else zags, and not merely pay lip service to the idea of zigging through a calculated PR plan built on convincing the fan base their approach is novel when it actually apes most of their competitors. Instead they've become far more concerned with making safe, accepted-by-the-new-common-wisdom decisions, such that our prior understanding of what a moral hazard is has become inverted.

I can't blame them entirely, and not only because of the reasons that Quinton illuminated in his article, but also because of the damage wrought by the introduction of the second wild card (WC2) spot. MLB's desire to have more teams in playoff contention has sparked anti-competitive behavior. Teams know now that they do not need to swing big as they assemble their roster because there is a good chance that a mediocre team can either catch fire and capture a division, or muddle along until they back into the WC2.

Simultaneously, the one-game playoff has neutered the WC1, putting an entire season on the flip of a coin like some sort of baseball-obsessed Anton Chigurh. While the one-game playoff makes sense as a way to increase the value of winning a division, it also means that if a front office doesn't like its chances of overcoming a behemoth like the Dodgers or Astros in the offseason, they have few incentives to chase glory. Similarly, the relative inaction in the NL Central at the trade deadline—despite a wide open division—can be explained by the idea that any high-variance investment could still result in only a wild card (or worse) result, given the mere two months left in the season to make an impact.

⚾ ⚾ ⚾

As stated at the top, we should not confuse reasons for excuses. The implementation of the second wild card is just one of many environmental factors that influence how each front office operates. I am convinced that it is one of the larger factors, but I am also convinced that organizations need to shed the yoke of "efficiency at all costs" so that they can instead pursue competition, as the spirit of the game intends. Until they do, we're all deadline losers.

—*Craig Goldstein is an author of Baseball Prospectus.*

Index of Names

Allen, Austin 70	Holmes, Grant 88, 100
Allen, Nick 71, 94	Howard, Brian 88
Armenteros, Lazaro 72, 99	Hurtado, Jhenderson 88
Barrera, Luis 86, 101	Jefferies, Daulton 83, 97
Barreto, Franklin 18	Kaprielian, James 84, 101
Bassitt, Chris 44	Kemp, Tony 28
Baum, Tyler 81, 102	Laureano, Ramón 30
Beck, Austin 73, 94	Luzardo, Jesus 85, 91
Blackburn, Paul 88	Manaea, Sean 56
Bolt, Skye 86, 102	Mateo, Jorge 78, 95
Brito, Marcos 74	McCann, Kyle 86
Brown, Seth 86	McFarland, T.J. 58
Buchter, Ryan 46	McIntyre, Aiden 88
Canha, Mark 20	Mengden, Daniel 88
Chapman, Matt 22	Montas, Frankie 60
Davidson, Logan 75, 98	Murphy, Sean 32, 93
Davis, Khris 24	Murray, Kyler 79
Deichmann, Greg 86, 102	Neuse, Sheldon 34, 98
Diaz, Jordan 76	Olson, Matt 36
Diekman, Jake 48	Pantuso, Alexander 104
Dunshee, Parker 82	Petit, Yusmeiro 62
Eierman, Jeremy 77, 103	Pinder, Chad 38
Estrada, Marco 88	Piscotty, Stephen 40
Fiers, Mike 50	Puason, Robert 80, 96
Fowler, Dustin 86	Puk, A.J. 64, 92
Goins, Ryan 86	Rivas, Alfonso 100
Grossman, Robbie 26	Romero, Miguel 88
Harvey, Matt 52	Schultz, Jaime 88
Heim, Jonah 86, 103	Semien, Marcus 42
Hendriks, Liam 54	Shreve, Chasen 88
Herrmann, Chris 86	Smith, Marcus 86, 104

Oakland Athletics 2020

Soria, Joakim 66
Trivino, Lou 68
Varland, Gus 88
Wendelken, J.B. 88